Advance Praise for *Exit Rich*

"It's stunning that so many business owners end up leaving so much equity on the table when they want to cash out. That's why this book will be a goldmine for these entrepreneurs."

STEVE FORBES—Chairman and Editor-In-Chief, *Forbes*

"Seiler Tucker's golden nuggets are priceless . . . a must-read for helping you build, fix, and grow your business so it's sellable for maximum value!"

DAVID MELTZER—Top Executive Business Coach and Keynote Speaker, CEO and Founder of Sports 1 Marketing

"If you're ready to build your business the right way so you can exit smart, then read and absorb the strategies in this brilliant book by Michelle and Sharon. The strategies will change your business and life!"

JAMES MALINCHAK—Featured on ABC's hit TV show, "Secret Millionaire;" Founder of BigMoneySpeaker.com

"Finally, a business book that helps entrepreneurs with practical strategies to maximize their exit. *Exit Rich* packs years of practical experience into a book that pays for itself ten times over."

JAY SAMIT—Best-selling Author of *Disrupt You!*

"Ever wonder why 70% of businesses go out of business after being in business for ten years? Seiler Tucker unravels the mystery in her 'tell all' book, all while delivering a proven formula so your business does not become a failing statistic."

DR. GREG REID—Author, Think and Grow Rich series

"*Exit Rich* reveals the BEST way to plan your company exit. It accounts for all steps from scaling to selling. The game plan is all laid out. All you have to do is follow it!"

LORAL LANGEMEIER—Best-selling Author,
Speaker, Millionaire Mentor

"The '6 P Method' is a concrete, quantifiable way to account for the added value of a business. This is a GREAT method to increase value and sell your business for HUGE profit, compared to the many traditional methods that don't really work. A must-read."

JEFF HOFFMAN—Global Entrepreneur from
Priceline.com and uBid.com

"Entrepreneurs take note! Yes, you want to make an impact with your business, but you also want to build it into a valuable asset in the process. Toward that end, Seiler Tucker's Golden Nuggets are priceless. This is a must read in helping you build, fix and grow your enterprise so it's sellable for maximum value!"

STEVE FARBER—Founder and CEO,
The Extreme Leadership Institute; Author,
The Radical Leap and Love Is Just Damn Good Business

"The ST GPS Exit is genius! It helps business owners plan their exit from the beginning so they can exit smart, exit rich, and exit on their terms!"

CHERYL SNAPP CONNER—CEO of SnappConner PR;
Creator of Content University™;
Entrepreneur Contributor, Author, and Speaker

"Anyone looking to sell their business would be smart to read *Exit Rich* to learn and apply the combined wisdom and experience of Sharon Lechter and Michelle Seiler Tucker."

DINA DWYER-OWENS—Past Chairman and CEO,
Neighborly Brands

"Sharon Lechter And Michelle Seiler Tucker have led faculty at CEO SPACE on the wealth missing CEO software 1.7 billion small business owners require. Their wisdom is finally available now for less than $10,000 in live classes—in *Exit Rich*. As founder of the largest small business community in the world, it is my opinion *Exit Rich* is the missing essential toolkit to turn your dreams into millions from the lady-leaders who have assisted countless CEOs and professionals to actually *do it*!"

BERNY DOHRMANN—Founder of CEO SPACE,
Author of *Super Change*

"When it comes to selling your business, there's a lot of different advice you can listen to, but the '6 P Method' Seiler Tucker and Lechter share in *Exit Rich* will actually work!"

DAVID M. CORBIN—*Wall Street Journal*
Best-selling Author, Mentor to Mentors

"*Exit Rich* reveals the best way to plan your company exit. Michelle and Sharon cover all of the steps and lay out the game plan from scaling to selling. All you have to do is follow it!"

ALEC STERN—Entrepreneur, Speaker, Mentor, Investor;
"America's Startup Success Expert"

An Inc. Original
New York, New York
www.anincoriginal.com

This work is being published under the An Inc. Original imprint by an exclusive arrangement with Inc. Magazine. Inc. Magazine and the Inc. logo are registered trademarks of Mansueto Ventures, LLC. The An Inc. Original logo is a wholly owned trademark of Mansueto Ventures, LLC.

Distributed by Greenleaf Book Group

For ordering information or special discounts for bulk purchases, please contact Greenleaf Book Group at PO Box 91869, Austin, TX 78709, 512.891.6100.

Design and composition by Greenleaf Book Group
Cover design by Greenleaf Book Group
Cover and interior images used under license from Shutterstock.com.
©Shutterstock.com/StockAppeal; ©Shutterstock.com/macrowildlife.

Publisher's Cataloging-in-Publication data is available.

Print ISBN: 978-1-7325102-8-9

eBook ISBN: 978-1-7325102-9-6

Part of the Tree Neutral® program, which offsets the number of trees consumed in the production and printing of this book by taking proactive steps, such as planting trees in direct proportion to the number of trees used: www.treeneutral.com

Printed in the United States of America on acid-free paper

20 21 22 23 24 25   10 9 8 7 6 5 4 3 2 1

First Edition

This book is dedicated to the clients of Seiler Tucker Incorporated. Thank you for giving us the honor and pleasure of serving you. Thanks for trusting us with selling your most prized possession, your business.

And a big thank you to the Seiler Tucker Team. You could choose to work anywhere; I am forever grateful that you chose Seiler Tucker as your career path, as your home. The STI team's contribution is what helps make us the best M&A firm in the nation.

Most importantly, this book is dedicated to my hero, my husband, Dr. Richard Anthony Tucker; and my beautiful, intelligent, and loving daughter, Arabella Acheanna Tucker. You both are my heart, my soul, my love, my everything!

"If you're trying to create a company, it's like baking a cake. You have to have all the ingredients in the right proportion."

—ELON MUSK

PART 3: SELLING YOUR BUSINESS

I s it time to sell your business? Maybe, maybe not. But it is never too early to start positioning your business to sell sometime in the future. And, it is best to have a guide to help you attract the highest price possible when it is time to sell. *Exit Rich* provides your road map to maximum profits. Michelle Seiler Tucker, the nation's leading M&A advisor, and Sharon Lechter, a global expert in financial literacy and a business mentor, have joined forces to combine their tremendous experience in order to provide you with the quintessential guide to selling your business at the highest profit possible.

You have undoubtedly worked hard to build your business. You've poured your expertise, your resources, and your time into it. Face it, deciding to sell it is a very emotional decision. Being overly excited and proud of what you have built can cause you to demand a price that is unrealistically high. On the other hand, being stressed or anxious might cause you to settle for a price that is much too low. In either case, you will benefit from having an expert advisor and advocate who is not encumbered with emotion.

You may have decided that you need to sell for personal reasons (age, health, retirement) or you may want to sell for business reasons (business needs an influx of capital or new management to continue to grow). Some of the more common reasons owners sell their businesses include:

- Owner burnout
- New opportunities

- Health reasons

- Partner disputes

- Declining revenues

- Unmanageable growth

- No children to inherit it

- Lifestyle changes

No matter what the reason you have for wanting to sell your business, there is a proven process you need to follow to prepare for your potential buyer. They will want to review not only your industry and competition, but also the history of your company and its current financial position. Our experience is that they will want to inspect just about every aspect of your business. And the better prepared you are, the greater the likelihood of your successful outcome.

According to the International Business Brokers Association, 90% of businesses listed for sale will *not* sell. While you are definitely an expert in your business, you are most likely not an expert in brokering businesses, and that's why you'll do well to read and take notes from this book. In *Exit Rich*, Michelle and Sharon show you how to establish maximum value within your company, from streamlining your operations, to identifying and protecting intellectual property, to handling personnel and business issues throughout the due diligence and sales process. They also help you understand from the buyer's perspective what will make your business most attractive for purchase.

Every business owner will benefit from studying *Exit Rich*, where Michelle and Sharon reveal the action steps you can take immediately to increase the value of your business.

KEVIN HARRINGTON
Founder of *As Seen on TV*
Best-Selling Author
Original Investor Shark on *Shark Tank*
www.kevinharrington.tv

Exit Rich

Business ownership is the backbone of our economic society. Generational wealth is most often created when a business owner sells his or her business at the right time, to the right buyer, at the maximum price. Unfortunately, too many people who have the entrepreneurial dream and start building their dream business fail to properly create the underlying foundation, systems, and structure that ensure their business is not only successful but also sustainable, scalable, and salable!

Michelle Seiler Tucker has created the perfect road map not only to help you build a successful business but also to package it to make it attractive to the perfect buyer. By following Michelle's formula, you will command the highest price possible when you decide to sell your business.

As one of America's leading mergers and acquisitions (M&A) advisors and business brokers, Michelle and her team have helped hundreds of business owners maximize the value and the sales prices for their businesses. In creating highly successful exits for her clients, she realized she could help so many more business owners by sharing her proprietary processes in this book.

Her Seiler Tucker GPS Exit Model®, as well as her 6 P Method®, have proven successful in many industries and across multiple business platforms.

Every bit of her advice has created a proven track record when successfully followed by her clients, making Michelle and her team stand out among the top M&A advisors and business brokers in America.

I was thrilled when Michelle and her business asked me if I would like to co-author this book with her. I have spent decades building, buying, and selling businesses and have had several successful exits from businesses I helped build. More importantly, I have mentored hundreds of business owners on these exact topics. As a financial literacy expert for the AICPA (American Institute of Certified Public Accountants) and a member of the Presidential Financial Literacy Advisory Council for both Presidents Bush and Obama, I am honored to be called upon as a recognized voice for entrepreneurship and business ownership internationally.

I was impressed with Michelle's track record, as well as how she works with her clients. You will find a section at the end of each chapter called the Mentoring Corner, where I add my expertise, experience, and guidance and highlight the importance of seeking advice from the right experts with proven track records.

Every business owner should read and adopt the advice from *Exit Rich*. It is my sincere hope that you will enjoy and profit from the wisdom shared here.

SHARON LECHTER
CPA, CGMA

ACKNOWLEDGMENTS

I was inspired and motivated to write this book by my peers, clients, and family. Most importantly, I was truly inspired to write this book because of the huge shift in today's business landscape. It used to be that 85–95 percent of all new ventures went out of business in the first five years. Now, the business climate has dramatically changed; only 30 percent will go out of business in the first five years, but a whopping 70 percent will go out of business after ten years. This statistic is a huge change that has occurred since writing my last book. I was inspired to write *Exit Rich* because, unfortunately, so many business owners are exiting poor! When an owner goes out of business, they don't only lose their business assets; they lose their family assets as well. It is my mission to help save as many of these businesses and their family wealth as humanly possible.

A big thanks to Sharon Lechter, *New York Times* best-selling co-author of *Rich Dad Poor Dad* and fourteen other Rich Dad books. She is also the author of *Think and Grow Rich for Women* and co-author of *Three Feet from Gold*, *Outwitting the Devil*, and *Success and Something Greater*, all in cooperation with the Napoleon Hill Foundation. Sharon is a true role model, an amazing entrepreneur, a financial literacy and personal growth expert, a captivating speaker, and an inspiration to us all.

I would also like to thank my good friend and mentor, David Corbin, who was instrumental in assisting me throughout my journey.

Most importantly, I would like to thank my husband, Dr. Richard Tucker, for his love, support, and encouragement. Dr. Tucker is a successful entrepreneur and truly gives back to the community.

My true inspiration and biggest motivation comes from my daughter, Arabella Acheanna Tucker. Selling and saving companies is truly my passion; however, raising my beautiful daughter is my everything. At the age of nine, Arabella is already becoming an entrepreneur, and she will hopefully continue to walk in Mommy's and Daddy's footsteps and create her own footprints along the way.

Finally, I would like to thank the reader. My hope is that you will find *Exit Rich* to be extremely informative and beneficial. I look forward to helping you navigate the delightful challenges of fixing and growing your business, using the Seiler Tucker proven systems, as well as planning your GPS Exit and selling your business for huge profits!

To your continued success and exiting rich, exiting smart, and exiting on your own terms!

MICHELLE SEILER TUCKER
M&AMI, CSBA, CM&AP, CBB

Exit Rich, Smart, and on Your Terms

Many people tell me that the best decision they ever made, by far, was starting or buying their own businesses. That is my story as well. Other than deciding to marry my husband and then have our daughter, it was the best decision I ever made. But it wasn't always so.

I used to have a position in corporate America, working for Xerox. I thought it was my dream come true: I was a top salesperson, and I was promoted to a position I thought I wanted, that of a high-volume manager, overseeing eighty salespeople. I was earning a healthy six-figure income with tremendous benefits. Within a few months, however, I felt dissatisfaction and dismay. And it finally hit me why.

I was making a ton of money for someone else. That made no sense to me. Plus, my team was out there selling, not me. I realized I was no longer doing what I loved. I wasn't selling. I wasn't solving my clients' problems, and I was no longer building relationships with those clients.

As the old adage states, "Be careful what you wish for." Instead of the thrill of the deal, I was dealing with corporate bureaucracy and company politics and babysitting a bunch of unruly salespeople. Believe me when I say one of the worst things a company can do is promote a top salesperson into management. Xerox learned that the hard way with me.

Hundreds of thousands of Americans stay in miserable jobs and complain to other people who are most likely also miserable. That's not me, so I decided to stop being miserable making money for someone else and become my own boss.

STARTING MY OWN BUSINESS

I knew my strengths and weaknesses. I knew what I was good at and what I loved to do. But I didn't want to start just any business. It had to be one that was heavily involved in sales and solving problems. I love the thrill of the deal, building relationships that last a lifetime, and solving my clients' problems. Whatever business I bought would have to make all that possible.

I found a struggling company in the early stages of selling franchises. It had a cookie-cutter formula, a training program, a small administrative support team, and brick-and-mortar stores. When I approached them about buying a franchise, they shared they were having trouble selling them. They did not want to sell me a franchise. Instead, they wanted me to partner with them in selling their franchises to others. After numerous meetings and conducting my due diligence, I negotiated an agreement to join forces with the owners, which led to starting my own franchise development company—and the ultimate departure from my "dream position."

At the time, my colleagues, friends, and family thought I was insane. One person even went so far as to say, "Who gives up a six-figure position—with phenomenal benefits? Are you nuts?" This decision certainly wasn't nuts. Sure, it might have appeared to a nonentrepreneur that to start a franchise development company and then collaborate with a company to sell the very franchises it couldn't sell on its own was bonkers. However, I didn't listen to their negativity and unsolicited advice. Instead, I leapt and never looked back. (Well, not never. I am looking back now with a big smile on my face!)

Within six months, I knew I had made a great decision. I was doing what I loved: selling franchises and generating more income per transaction than what I made the entire year at my corporate job. But then my situation changed.

After selling franchises for a few years, I found myself in a quandary. My philosophy—underpromise and overdeliver—was not in synch with that of my franchise partner; it was actually the opposite. They couldn't fulfill the packages of service, training, and support that I was selling to our franchisees. Instead of solving my clients' problems, I was creating them. I couldn't continue to work that way.

I then started my own mergers and acquisitions (M&A) firm, specializing in buying and selling businesses, as well as new and existing franchises. I started doing exactly what I loved to do: helping my sellers plan exit strategies and sell their businesses at their desired price. I sold hundreds of businesses. In addition, I was helping buyers obtain financial freedom by becoming their own bosses and achieving a better quality of life.

Since opening my M&A firm, startling statistics have caused me to realize and fine-tune my real passion of saving businesses and of saving the owners and their families from losing their personal assets. Unfortunately, eight out of ten businesses do not sell, for a multitude of reasons. This is horrible news for most business owners because many of them will have to sell their business for pennies on the dollar, close their doors, and—even worse—file for bankruptcy and lose everything!

These outcomes are beyond sad to me. These business owners dedicated their lives to building their business and made huge sacrifices. Baby boomers facing these challenges, in particular, may not have the runway left in their lives to rebuild.

To address these issues, I have directed my focus into developing my Build to Sell program, which helps business owners build their business to sell for millions. I invest my expertise, resources, time, energy, effort, and sometimes money in partnering with many business owners to build their business to sell to one of our existing buyers who is willing to pay top dollar for good businesses. In addition, I have created an M&A and business brokerage training program that is unparalleled in the industry. This program teaches up-and-coming M&A advisors and business brokers everything

PART 1

PLANNING YOUR EXIT

1

The ST GPS Exit Model®: How to Create Your Exit When You Begin

"I can't change the direction of the wind,
but I can adjust my sails to always reach my destination."

—Jimmy Dean

L et's face it: Rarely does someone go into business with the end game in mind. Think back to when you started or bought your business. You were probably beyond the moon excited to be your own boss, able to create your own financial freedom and to have more quality time to spend with your family. However, those dreams became overshadowed rather quickly by the overwhelming demands of building and running your business—or, worse yet, your business running you!

The biggest issue I see with business owners is that they don't plan their exit, or end game, when they launch their business. Even when they do plan on selling their company eventually, they usually haven't determined their desired sales price or range. Sadly, most entrepreneurs and franchise owners don't think of selling until they're forced to due to boredom, poor performance, or a catastrophic event. These, unsurprisingly, are usually the worst times to sell. The best time to sell is when your business is doing well and trending up.

BUILD YOUR PERFECT SALE WITH THE ST GPS EXIT MODEL®

At Seiler Tucker, we specialize in working with business owners early in their entrepreneurial journey so they can identify the perfect time to exit their business. To do so, we use the ST GPS Exit Model. This is a step-by-step process that should be the blueprint of how the business is built from the day you buy or start your company. This model will help you create the framework or context for building, scaling, and selling your company, and this context will help you keep your effort and energies focused on your desired end game.

THE ST GPS EXIT MODEL

1. Determine your destination (desired sales price).

2. Know your current location (the value of your company).

3. Identify who your buyers will be.

4. Know your time frame.

5. Determine your WHY.

GPS EXIT STEP 1: DETERMINE YOUR DESTINATION

The first thing you need to do is establish a goal by determining the amount you want to sell your business for. This is when you need to think about what sales price will make you happy while staying true to the actual value of the company. Almost every business owner comes to us with a price in mind that they want to sell their business for; however, that price is usually based on hopes and dreams. It's typically based on the amount they need to get out of debt or to use for the next chapter of their lives. Unfortunately, most sellers don't determine their destination. Instead, they navigate their business without a road map, driving aimlessly in circles, hitting bumps, landing in ditches, and going up and down the financial hills until many of them simply run out of gas, hit rock bottom, and get flipped upside down in debt.

We have seen business owners lead their company for years and end up running it into the ground due to mistakes or bad decisions along the way (either their own mistakes or mistakes outside of their control). When this occurs, the business becomes difficult or impossible to sell, and it certainly won't sell for the price that the seller needs to move forward or to get out of debt related to the business.

Years ago, I met with the owners of a manufacturing company who wanted to sell their business. These owners said they wanted to sell their company for $5 million. I said, "Okay, how did you come up with that number?" They told me that's how much they had in inventory, furniture, fixtures, and equipment, and that's what they needed to pay off their debt. I explained to them that the price of the business has nothing to do with what they owe. Instead, it's determined by the cash flow from the business. In other words, the profitability must support a price of $5 million for the business to be worth $5 million.

Our firm performed an evaluation and discovered that this business was making about $50,000 a year. Their wish price of $5 million equated to ten times the amount of the value they were bringing in. Industry standards and comps would support a price three to four times the amount of their EBITDA (earnings before interest, taxes, depreciation, and amortization), but not ten. We were obviously worlds apart on price. We based our valuation on industry standards, comps, and the Buyer's Sanity Check, whereas the owner had based their price on what they needed to pay off their debt and have some money left over. However, they didn't yet know about the ST GPS Exit Model discussed here.

The true sales price of a business is not based on what its owners need to pay off their debt or live on; it's based on how many cylinders a company operates on and how profitable it is. At the end of the day, cash flow must support the asking price and meet the buyer's needs. These owners ended up not selling, because they could not afford to sell and pay off their debt; even worse, they ended up filing for bankruptcy.

Unfortunately, there are numerous stories like this one. The buyer will not base their offer number on what you owe or what you need to live on; they simply base their offer on what they feel your business is worth and how soon they can obtain an ROI if they purchase your company. This is why the most important step in the beginning stages of your business is knowing what your desired end game is and what your future sale should look like. If you don't do this in the beginning, you could lose your business and family assets in the process. However, doing it will also give you a road map to follow as you grow your business. For example, if you want to sell your company for $20 million, you must build a $20 million company. This can sound simple, but it takes a tremendous amount of work. You'll need to know what a $20 million company looks like. You need to know their gross revenues, their EBITDA, what their management team does, and how their company functions.

GPS EXIT STEP 2: KNOW YOUR CURRENT VALUE

It's imperative to know your destination. You will never drive to your business's destination without knowing where you started from—your current valuation. We call this a valuation checkup. You must work with an expert M&A advisor or business broker on an annual basis to look under the hood of your business, determine your current value, and inspect your value drivers (known as the ST 6 P's® which we will cover in part 2). After the inspection, you must tune up what's necessary to drive on the path to your final destination.

Most business owners do not get their business valued until they are thinking about selling it. This is typically where the rubber meets the road and the M&A advisor or business broker usually has to inform the owner that their baby is not as pretty as they thought and that it won't sell for their desired sales price, because it's not performing at maximum value, its valuation of assets are unrealistic, and the cash flow does not support their dream price.

It baffles us how people will get their car inspected and get an annual health checkup, but they completely ignore the health of their business until they are ready to sell. In most cases, our business is our most prized possession. It's our nest egg, our retirement plan, but it's also the most neglected asset we have. Because of this, we need to check on it throughout its lifetime—not just at selling time. We don't have many business owners who come to us for an annual valuation. Most come to us only when they are ready to sell. Unfortunately, that may be too late; their business is not usually sellable, for a multitude of reasons.

To know the current health of your business, you'll need to engage with an experienced professional. We encourage you to do so from the infancy stage of your business. This professional can perform valuations, inspections, and tune-ups to build a well-oiled machine that buyers are willing to pay top dollar for when the time comes for you to sell.

GPS EXIT STEP 3: KNOW WHO YOUR BUYERS WILL BE

When entrepreneurs start or buy a business, they typically do their due diligence and determine who their ideal customer is. Smart owners will do market research to determine their clients' demographics, such as their age, gender, income, and buying habits. They create a sales model with products and services that fill a void, servicing a niche with their target audience in mind. The owners will do it themselves or hire a marketing firm to create specific media campaigns to reach and inspire their ideal buyers to purchase their goods and services.

Business owners invest their money, energy, and resources to target their ideal customer and entice them to purchase their goods. So why would they not invest as much in targeting the ideal buyers that will one day purchase their most prized possession, their business, and then build the business to suit those buyers' specific buying criteria? Business owners would have such an advantage if they simply planned their exit from the very beginning. To do this, you'll need to know what buyers are looking for and build your business to suit their specific buying criteria. The formula is easier than most sellers realize. Simply follow the steps in determining who your best client for selling your business is, and build your business to suit that investor's specific buying criteria. It's important to conduct your due diligence from the beginning. Research your industry, know who your competitors are, and find out who's buying them. You'll want to find out the details about the business's operations, including the amount the buyer paid, the structure of the business, the seller's gross revenues, and the EBITDA.

You can also consult with an M&A advisor or business broker early on and pick their brain. Ask them who your buyers might be, and inquire about the industry standards and business comps that they'd be most impressed by. Determine the answers to this question: What are the buyer's criteria? That is, what does the potential buyer want as it relates to industry, financials, business location, business operation, and business size?

Most advisors will be able to tell you the buyer's target revenue, cash flow, business size, type of management team, and operations. They should work with you to determine your ideal suitor and help you design and build the company to meet that buyer's criteria. It's imperative to determine who your buyer will be and build your business to suit that buyer's specific needs. To help with this, we will explore the five different types of buyers in golden nugget 4. The following case study demonstrates the various types of attributes buyers may be looking for.

EXAMPLE: A BUSINESS IN
THE MANUFACTURING INDUSTRY

What groups buy manufacturing?
   PEGs (private equity groups), strategic or competitor buyers
What is the gross revenue requirement?
   $15,000,000–$20,000,000
What is the EBITDA requirement?
   $1,000,000–$3,000,000
What is the management requirement?
   A strong management team, including a COO and a CFO

---

continued

What are the operation requirements?

Operating on all six cylinders, also known as the 6 P Method

Where are the business locations?

They are open to buying anywhere in the United States.

What is the average multiple that determines price?

Four to six times EBITDA

What assets are included?

Furniture, fixtures, and equipment (FF&E), accounts receivable, real estate, working capital, all proprietary

What is the typical structure?

Asset sale, 60 to 70 percent down; seller could retain equity, seller financing, possible earnout on the upside; seller pays off all debt and possibly accounts payable

Examples like this can be great road maps to follow when you're making decisions in the present that can set you up to sell your business for your desired sales price down the line. The big takeaway here is that you need to engage an expert to determine your ideal buyers and their buying criteria. After you do this, you can build to suit to their specific needs and wants. This will help you earn huge profits when you are ready to sell your business.

GPS EXIT STEP 4: KNOW YOUR TIME FRAME

Timing is everything. Once you have determined your desired sales price and your buyer's criteria, you need to determine the time frame in which to build your business so it can sell for your desired sales price. Your objective to sell your business cannot be achieved without strategically determining this.

Timing will be different depending on the person and the business. For example, a younger business owner might decide that they want to retire when they are fifty or sixty, and that could be a twenty- to thirty-year time frame. However, if a business owner is in their fifties, they may have a ten-year time frame. When we partner with or buy a business, we typically want to dominate the market and sell for our desired price tag in five to seven years. If an owner is in an industry that they see as dying and/or being replaced with technology, they may decide to exit within a year or two. It's all relative and depends on a person's age, the economy, and their appetite for wanting to exit so they can create their next masterpiece.

GPS EXIT STEP 5: DETERMINE YOUR WHY

It's natural to set goals. Unfortunately, however, many people never achieve them. Perhaps they have not set a specific written goal, or they have not set a specific time frame. Most importantly and most likely, they have not identified their WHY. It's important to determine your WHY for wanting to sell your business for your desired price in your specified time frame.

Setting goals is easy; however, actually accomplishing them can be more difficult. Let's face it: If it were easy to sell your business for $50 million, everyone would do it, right? However, most business owners will not obtain their dream price, because they left out the most important ingredient: their WHY. You can't bake a cake without flour. If you did, your cake would never rise. The same holds true with your business. If you leave out the key ingredient, your WHY, the sales price will never rise to your desired expectations.

THE RULES OF GOAL SETTING

To keep focused on your WHY, it is important to set goals for your business. Goals will keep you moving forward. The rules of goal setting are simple:

1. Define a specific goal.

2. Set a time frame to accomplish your goal.

3. Determine your WHY.

It's almost impossible to set goals when you are unclear of what you really want in your life. Setting meaningful goals takes some serious soul-searching to determine what you really want to accomplish in your business and personal life. Most of us entrepreneurs are super busy running our businesses, tending to our families, and handling life's everyday occurrences. It's hard to determine what your ultimate goals are when you are so overwhelmed on a daily basis. Therefore, it's imperative to take some time to escape the noise and try and do some deep meditation and soul-searching to determine what you really want.

There are three types of goals that you should consider:

A-Type Goals

A-type goals are the goals you know you can reach with little to no effort, because you have done it before. There are no real hurdles to overcome, and there is absolutely no growth in obtaining these goals. For example, let's say your goal is to buy a newer version of the car you currently drive. You can set a specific goal: to buy a new, fully loaded BMW X5. Next, set the time frame: February of next year. Then, discover your WHY: the desire for a new, nicer car. The WHY is not a particularly strong desire, nor is this goal a vehicle for real growth if you already drive a BMW X4, for example.

B-Type Goals

B-type goals take a little more effort, but they are obtainable. It may help you grow a little to pursue a B-type goal, but it won't push you to learn new skills or challenge you to grow outside your comfort level.

For example, say you live in a 4,000-square-foot house in a nice neighborhood and you want to buy a new house. You can set a specific goal: to buy a 6,000-square-foot house in an exclusive gated community. Next, set the time frame: within one year. Then, discover your WHY: the desire for a nicer home.

As you can gather, this goal will take more effort than buying a new BMW, but it's not going to be so difficult that it causes you to necessarily grow and get outside of your comfort level. You need to determine your WHY and put together a plan to accomplish this goal in your desired time frame. However, this type of goal is not going to stretch you beyond your current capabilities.

C-Type Goals

C-type goals are those goals that are completely outside your reach, and you have no idea how you are going to accomplish them. C-type goals are what excite us, what get our juices flowing, and what keep us in the game, no matter how difficult the obstacles are. These are the goals that have invented electricity, the Internet, and smartphones. These are the goals that changed the world. They are not easily obtained, but like the lesser goals, they must be specific, have assigned time frames, and—most importantly—encompass a defined WHY.

Beware, though. Your C-type goals will be full of distractions, roadblocks, potholes, and crashes. As a result, you must identify and stay true to your WHY and stay on course, despite everyone and everything that is trying to deter you and knock you off your path.

If your C-type goals do not scare you, you are not reaching high enough. You might be saying, "I don't have all the answers, competency, or skill sets; therefore, I will never reach my C-type goals." On the contrary, if you know all the answers, you are on the wrong path, and you won't experience any growth along the way. Once your C-type goals are clear, the magic happens, the specialist appears, answers show up, and a path is created.

Selling a business for millions or even billions of dollars in a specific time frame is a definite C-type goal, and it works best when there is a WHY. Typically, three to six months after the engagement process begins, sellers have this middle-of-the-night epiphany about what they want to do with the next chapter of their lives. Their new idea might strike like a bolt of lightning, but it has actually been there for a long time, buried under the weight of their obligations. Once a seller feels that it's okay to sell, they can start thinking of themselves and what they would like to do next. Often, this is almost impossible to do by yourself when you are in the weeds of indecision. However, when you drive down the exit path and follow all five steps of the ST GPS Exit Model, you will set yourself and your family up for true success by exiting smart, exiting rich, and exiting on your own terms.

MENTORING CORNER

Additional insights are provided throughout this book from business mentor Sharon Lechter's perspective, to add additional context and insight for the business owner.

There are many reasons for starting a business. Some people want

continued

to create generational wealth, whereas others just want to make a living. Then there are people who simply enjoy the strategic aspects of building a business and others who enjoy participating in business operations. And then there are the serial entrepreneurs, who simply enjoy the startup and the early stages of building a business.

No matter what your reasons for starting a business, when it comes time to sell, it is not your desires or expectations but, rather, the value of your business as perceived by the buyer that counts. This means that you need to package your business, laying the foundation for maximum perceived evaluation, by generating high sustainable cash flow, as well as creating high asset valuation. You can also create what Michael Lechter refers to as "demonstrative assets," things that tend to serve as evidence to the underlying value of otherwise intangible assets. Depending on the circumstances of your business, these can include patents, trademark, and copyright registrations and a fortress of contracts preventing the appropriation of your secret sauce and business relationships. These items warrant consideration in the stages of your business startup and growth to set you up for a successful sale at maximum value.

Sadly, many small businesses fail to lay the foundation to capitalize on potential intellectual property assets or fail to recognize those valuable intellectual property assets that they may have as they are growing their company. They may not have patented or registered trademarks but may well have valuable know-how and expertise, unregistered trademarks, and goodwill. These intangible assets could be worth millions in valuation and sales price.

This is another important reason to have a mentor or advisor—to help keep your emotions in check. I have a saying: "High emotion means low intelligence." You have spent years starting and growing your business; it will be an emotional journey to go through the process of selling it, even if you are excited by the idea.

You may think your business is worth much more than a realistic valuation will produce. That fact alone creates great stress and emotion. You are not alone. It is seldom the case that a business owner thinks their business is worth less than the buyer is willing to offer.

Having a mentor or advisor to serve as a sounding board throughout the process is a huge benefit. Their advice and suggestions won't be

> clouded with emotion, and they will shine a more realistic light on the process. Their participation is even more important in the early stages, while your management team or employees are not aware of the potential for a sale.

KNOW MORE TO EXIT RICH

As you've learned in this chapter, it's not what you know that will get you in trouble; it's what you don't know that will get you in more trouble than you ever thought possible. And in some cases, it can cause irrevocable damage. However, if you set proper goals and follow all five rules of navigating your GPS Exit, you will set yourself up for success by exiting smart, exiting rich, and exiting on your own terms.

DID YOU KNOW?

- According to *Forbes*, eight out of ten businesses will not sell.

- According to the US Bureau of Labor Statistics, 70 percent of all businesses go out of business after being in operation for ten years.

- According to *Forbes*, in a recent survey of San Diego businesses, 53 percent of business owners had given little or no thought to their transition, despite the fact that three-fourths of the respondents were fifty-one or older.

- According to Abrigo, in a recently released survey on family-owned businesses, one-third of businesses who expected to have a change in ownership within the next five years had no plan for succession, and of those surveyed who did have a plan, only 23 percent had written it down.

IMPLEMENTATION IS KEY

To further explore the lessons learned in this chapter, implement the following:

- Define your ST GPS Exit Model.

- Determine your desired sales price.

- Know your current valuation or business worth.

- Know who your buyers will be.

- Build to suit your buyer's criteria.

- Know your time frame.

- Know your WHY.

- Align yourself with a trusted M&A advisor.

For more free special training, please visit SeilerTuckerAcademy.com to watch a video of Michelle explaining the ST GPS Exit Model.

2

Step into a Seller's Mindset: Why and When to Sell Your Business

"Time is an illusion, timing is an art."

—Stefan Emunds

One of the most difficult things for business owners is to know when to sell their business. Sellers typically don't think about selling their business until they have to or until a catastrophic event has occurred, leaving them without a choice and without a plan built with the ST GPS Exit Model. This, unfortunately, is usually the worst time to sell your business because, in most cases, it's trending downward. The best time to sell your business is when it's doing well and on the upswing.

Most people do not start or buy a business with their exit in mind. In fact, most business owners and entrepreneurs who decide to start or buy a business want to make a profit by solving a problem or serving a need. After awhile, they wake up and find themselves stuck in the day-to-day operations. They call themselves entrepreneurs, but what they really become are firefighters. In other words, instead of working on their business, they find themselves working *in* their business. Instead of owning a business, they own a job.

Many baby boomers who are long-time business owners often wake up one day and find that the passion for their work is gone. The challenges they faced when starting the company have been solved, and now, they are ready for the next chapter of their lives, so they decide they want to sell. These people have continuously sacrificed holidays, time with family, and money to get their business to where it is and working well. They've built and maintained great concepts, loyal customer bases, excellent name recognition, and brand awareness.

But now, even though they don't want to run their business anymore, they feel an obligation to continue for their families, employees, and clients, because they don't know what they want for themselves. They don't know how to move on from the work they've done for decades.

Selling your business—your life's work—is about more than profit. It's about realizing your dreams and achieving your WHY. Selling your business at the right time ensures that you have all the capital you need to move ahead with your life and do all the things you want to do, like start another business, retire, or even move to another country.

Do you know what you want next? That's a hard question, but it's an important first step in selling your business, because it's hard to close one chapter if you don't know how the next one begins. It can take a lot of soul-searching to figure that out.

Michelle worked with a couple who owned a business and constantly changed their minds about selling. One minute, they were for it; the next, they weren't. About six months into the sales process, the husband called her and said, "I've been struggling with selling all this time, because I didn't know what I was going to do with the rest of my life. Well, I had an epiphany last night, and now I have clarity. I know exactly what I'm going to do. We've always been passionate about bed and breakfasts, so we're going to use the proceeds from the sale to open our own B&B."

Once there was a reason for selling their business, they moved forward, getting maximum value for it. They're now running a successful B&B. Like many entrepreneurs who do what they love, they'd prefer to expire, not retire.

Typically, three to six months after the engagement process begins, sellers have this middle-of-the-night epiphany about what they want to do with the next chapter of their lives. Their "new" idea might strike like a bolt of lightning, but it has been there for a long time, buried under the weight of their obligations. Once a seller feels that it's okay to sell, they can start thinking of themselves and what they would like to do next. Often, though, this is almost impossible to do by yourself when you are in the weeds of indecision.

This is another way that having an M&A specialist advisor is useful. Perhaps one of the most important things an M&A specialist can do is help you realize what selling your business will enable you to accomplish. You can walk away from selling your business with a healthy profit and a lot of regret if you don't have a personally meaningful goal in place. But once you have that next step in mind, your advisor will work with you to prepare your exit strategy, the plan that ensures that your business ends up in good hands.

Those new B&B owners in the last example worked with an M&A specialist at Seiler Tucker to achieve their goal. We got them there by asking them two sets of questions. The first helped them identify what they wanted out of life; the second identified the selling issues they felt were important. Together, the answers enabled them to recognize whether an offer for their business would get them what they wanted.

DETERMINE YOUR GOALS

Figuring out your business goals doesn't have to be laborious or hard. Begin with this exercise for figuring out what you want and what your goals are.

Make two lists, as shown in the example below:

- In list 1, write all the things you no longer want in your life.
- In list 2, write down everything you want in your life.

THINGS I DON'T WANT IN MY BUSINESS OR LIFE	THINGS I DO WANT IN MY BUSINESS OR LIFE
I don't want to own my business anymore.	I want to own my life.
I don't want to work in my business anymore.	I want to work on my business or sell it.
I don't want to worry about my business 24/7.	I want to take stress-free, unencumbered vacations.
I don't want to deal with employees anymore.	I want to spend more time with my family.
I don't want the responsibility of owning my own business anymore.	I want to be free of the responsibility of owning my own business.
I don't want to be in debt.	I want to be debt free.
I don't want to be under stress.	I want to be stress free.

Completing this exercise should brighten the light at the end of the tunnel and clarify for you how much you have to look forward to after successfully selling your business. Your "don't want" list should solidify your WHY and identify steps to help eliminate the things you no longer want in your life.

We often tell people, when their lists are done, to tear up the "don't want" list and move on with their "want" goals. (Michelle tossed hers years ago and hasn't looked back.) From now on, focus only on your "want" list.

KNOW YOUR MARKET:
HOW TO GET INTO A SELLER'S MINDSET

When you're ready, take the second set of questions to evaluate an exit plan for your business based on the following important criteria: Will it enable you to accomplish what's on your "want" list? By answering the questions that follow, you will get into a seller's mindset and be well on your way to deciding on a plan for your sale.

THE SELLER'S SANITY CHECK

Use these questions to guide you in creating an exit plan with your M&A advisor:

- How much will my business sell for?
  - What's my tax liability?
  - How much do I owe?
  - How much do I walk away with?
- How much is my lifestyle on a monthly or annual basis?
- Will the proceeds of the sale enable me to afford my lifestyle?
  - How much will my lifestyle cost on a monthly or annual basis?
  - Will I have to get a job or find another company to buy?
- Where and what can I invest the money from the sale of my business or real estate in?
- Is my business going to be left in good hands?
  - Will the new owner keep and take good care of my employees?
  - Will they provide the same level of quality?
  - Will they take good care of my clients?
- Will my legacy continue to grow?

BE READY TO EXPLAIN WHY YOU'RE SELLING

Buyers always ask my firm, "What are the reasons businesses sell?" One of the most common questions buyers have is, "If the business is doing well, why would the owner sell?" We explain that businesses sell for a multitude of reasons—some good, some not. However, if we cannot answer that question to the buyer's satisfaction, in all likelihood, they won't buy the company. Buyers are always cautious about buying a struggling business that's about to become obsolete. They will require reps and warranties to ensure they are buying a good, sound business.

The first step of getting into a seller's mindset is to know your reason and be able to articulate it to buyers. Following are some of the main reasons most business owners decide to sell their companies.

COMMON REASONS BUSINESSES SELL

- The owner wants to retire.
- The owner or the owner's partner has health issues.
- There is a death of owner, partner, or family member.
- The owner is going through a divorce.
- The owner is relocating.
- The owner is burned out.
- The owner wants to go out and create their next masterpiece.
- The owner is tired of dealing with employees.
- The business is not doing well.
- The industry is dying.
- The kids do not want to take over the family business.

It's also just as important to know why you want to sell and what you're going to do next in order to prevent seller's remorse. One of the top reasons that businesses don't close is seller's remorse. Unfortunately, even when you think you have identified the reason to sell and the next chapter of your life, seller's remorse seems to creep back in, and it kills deals. This happens because sellers are comfortable in the current environment of running their company. The unknown is scary and uncomfortable. Therefore, I always tell my clients to get comfortable with being uncomfortable. Only in becoming uncomfortable can real growth and enjoyment take place!

MENTORING CORNER

HAVE AN EXIT STRATEGY

Being clear on why you are selling your business will help drive the best results. Most businesses start with a mission but fail to have an exit strategy in mind. They may have the goal of creating generational wealth, building a company that will provide for and be managed by future generations, or simply of enjoying the business and contemplating running it forever. At some point, however, for whatever reason, the founders will exit, either because there is a succession of management with the founders (or their estate) maintaining all or part of their ownership interest in the company or because the original founders simply cash out and sell their ownership interest.

DECIDE YOUR DESIRED TYPE OF SALE

When deciding on your exit strategy, you also want to consider the type of sale. Consider the following potential exit scenarios:

- A business owner chooses to sell while the business is strong and growing and still under his or her control.

- A business owner hires professional management and chooses to retire from the day-to-day operations, becoming a passive owner or board member.

- A business owner sells part of their ownership interest to investors that assume an active role in running the company, partially cashing out and relieving them of all or some of the responsibilities of running the business.

- A business owner wants to create generational wealth by building a company so it can provide for and be managed by future generations of their family.

continued

- A business owner chooses to sell the company to his or her management team or employees using an ESOP (employee stock ownership plan).

- A business owner takes the company public by going through a governmental disclosure approval process with the end goal of selling equity interests (shares) in the company to the public at large.

- A business owner uses an M&A advisor to grow the business and sell it for more.

Clearly, there are lots of options available that can permit the business owner to meet their own particular goals. A business owner can choose any or a combination of the above approaches. However, in any event, planning ahead and laying a proper foundation will facilitate accomplishing those goals.

Where the goal is to take cash out by selling all or part of the ownership of the business, timing and planning are of the essence. Without proper planning and timing of business decisions, the business owner runs the risk of the business he or she spent years building becoming a distressed business, which may end up not being salable at all.

A business owner can also choose a combination of the above approaches. While not appropriate for most businesses, we should mention another exit strategy that may be available to a business owner: taking the company public. With this strategy, the business owner navigates through a burdensome and costly governmental disclosure approval process, with the end goal of selling equity interests (shares) in the company to the public at large. This can provide a financial exit for the owner, while at the same time bringing in resources for future growth and, often, a professional management team to take the company into the future. While this option can sound exciting, in reality, it is extremely time consuming, costly, and feasible only for a small percentage of businesses. And even when successful, it creates significant administrative burden. It should not be entered into lightly.

WHEN MULTIPLE BUYERS MAY BE WARRANTED

Another thing to consider is whether you should entertain multiple buyers for specific products or industries. To do this successfully, you need to plan ahead and lay the foundation. For example, when we worked with the sale of a talking book company, we knew we had two separate lines of products that appealed to two different industries: the talking children's books business and a division of the company that sold sheet music. While getting ready to sell the company, we prepared financials dividing the company operating results between the two divisions. As a result, we were able to sell each division to separate interested buyers. While doing due diligence and negotiating with multiple buyers is difficult and time consuming, this helped us maximize the value received for the company, which outweighed the difficulty factor and extra time involved in the end.

TIMING

You have heard the saying "timing is everything," and it is true. Think about buying investment real estate. As a seller, you want to sell when the market is high, whereas as a buyer, you want to buy when the market is low. The magic of a good deal is when both buyer and seller agree to a negotiated price after a back and forth of offers and compromise. The same is true in selling your business.

Selling your business when your profits are on the rise gives you a much stronger position than when your business is suffering. In that same vein, if you are about to introduce a new profit center or new process that will create a much higher profit margin, you may want to wait until you can show the resulting positive impact to your bottom line, because it will increase the value of your business.

For example, we once counseled a client in the cement business to wait until a new process was employed for increasing productivity, as well as securing the new permitting he was working on that would allow him to mine materials to a depth of up to 100 feet instead of the forty feet he currently had permits for. Both moves would generate improved profitability and higher reserves—increased valuation—for his business. By waiting six more months, he was able to increase his company's valuation by millions of dollars.

According to *Business Insider*, most businesses take nearly two years to sell, from beginning to end. Don't go at it alone. Your mentor or M&A advisor can help you strategize the best time to consider selling your business and, often, will have the contacts and associations to bring the right resources to the table to assist you in maximizing your valuation at the time of sale.

KNOW MORE TO EXIT RICH

When getting ready to sell your business, it's important to do some deep soul-searching and to step into a seller's mindset. As we discussed, you can do this by determining your goals and knowing your market so that you can create an exit strategy that will work best for you.

DID YOU KNOW?

- According to *Business Insider*, it can take almost two years to sell a business.
- According to CNBC, many sellers hang on for a perfect time that never comes, losing sight that their goal should be a successful—not a perfect—sale.
- According to CNBC, it's common in family and small businesses to hear about seller's remorse, frequently because they haven't figured out what they'll do next.

IMPLEMENTATION IS KEY

To further explore the lessons learned in this chapter, implement the following:

- Use the Seller's Sanity Check to determine your goals for the sale.
- Ask yourself the seller's questions above to determine when you should start the sale process.
- Do some soul-searching, and identify the next chapter in your life.
- Think about what type of sale and buyer you'd prefer.

(3)

What Kind of Business Are You?

"A big business starts small."
—Richard Branson

N ow that you're clear on why you're selling your business, let's look at what you're selling. Ask yourself what kind of business you are. Business owners and entrepreneurs know it takes time, money, energy, and effort to build a business. Almost all new businesses show a loss at first and often don't show a profit for three to five years. Many new businesses realize too late that they don't have enough capital to last that long, which is why more than half fail in the first twelve months.

The longer you've been in business, weathering the storms, doing well, and making a good profit, the more you can maximize the value of your company. Established businesses are more attractive to buyers, because, as a general rule, they're less risky. However, not all businesses are equal. Depending on the type of business and its style of ownership, different advantages and risks appeal to different kinds of buyers.

When you are selling a company, the duration it's been in business is important; however, it's not as crucial as the relationship of its owner to the business. Some important questions to consider are whether the owner is so tied to their role in the company that the business wouldn't exist without them and whether there are processes and people in place that will allow the business to survive an ownership change.

ARE YOU SELLING A BUSINESS OR A JOB?

The sale of a business often depends on its ownership. For example, is the owner tied to the job in such a way that the business wouldn't exist without him or her? If so, you'll want to make sure that your business can survive without its current owner, that it clicks with the buyers, and that it's clear that it is a business, not a job. Different types of businesses attract different buyers. It's important to know your business category or what category you want your business to be in before you market your business for sale.

In the next chapter, we'll look at the five types of buyers, but right now, let's consider the basic business types and the ways in which they're run. It's important to know how your business may be categorized or how you want it to be classified before you market your business for sale. There are seven basic types of businesses:

- Dreamer businesses

- Established businesses

- Absentee businesses

- The one-man- or one-woman show

- Small businesses

- Small to medium companies

- Middle-market or larger companies

DREAMER BUSINESSES

We will begin by looking at what is probably the most common type of enterprise, the dreamer business. Many people start businesses based on their passions. They believe that if they do what they love, the money will follow. Much time and capital go into their business, because they're convinced their concept is so unique and exceptional that customers will come flocking to them.

Some people call beginning business owners like these "entrepreneurs." At Seiler Tucker, we call them dreamers. Dreamers set themselves up for failure, not success. Here's why the dreamer plan is flawed.

Most dreamers don't have experience running or starting a business. They do not know that they must take the time to research their markets, conduct due diligence, pull demographics, and create a business and marketing plan. The majority have done none of these things. If they had, they'd know that they're likely to have losses at first and probably won't realize a profit for years. As a result, they're severely undercapitalized. If they want to sell, the business isn't worth enough for the dreamer to recoup their investment.

Even with an enthusiastic buyer, dreamer businesses, like gift, coffee, and dress shops, are not going to sell for top dollar. Many of them lose money, so they're likely to sell for the value of their assets, including inventory and furniture, fixtures, and equipment (FF&E). A little cash flow, however, could sweeten the deal.

ESTABLISHED BUSINESSES

Even though established businesses have weathered the five-year startup period and are generally running well and heading into profitability, owners may still want to sell them for a variety of reasons:

- They have the seven-year itch, and they are true entrepreneurs and are bored with the business.
- They still have plenty of youthful energy, motivation, spirit, and fight left in them to go out and create their next masterpiece.

Established businesses that have been around for decades, owned either by a single individual or family or by multiple owners, are great to sell because they are inherently stable. They have a proven track record, have built a loyal client base, enjoy good profit, and, in the case of multiple owners, have been through the sale process. If cash is flowing through the business, they're worth a higher multiple, meaning they can sell for maximum profit.

ABSENTEE BUSINESS

If a true absentee-owner business existed, it would be in great demand. While so-called absentee businesses, such as Laundromats, storage facilities, car washes, trailer parks, and apartment complexes, don't require as much hands-on attention from the owner as other small businesses, they do require some. Many buyers want residual income without investing a lot of effort, so absentee businesses that show positive cash flow sell more quickly than all other small businesses.

However, it is important to note that absentee businesses don't all show positive cash flow, though, because some owners don't report their cash. This can create a huge problem with the IRS, which makes it nearly impossible to maximize value because there's no way to prove the income to a buyer.

THE ONE-MAN OR ONE-WOMAN SHOW

The one-man or one-woman show is 100 percent dependent on the owner being present every day. Without the owner, there is nothing to sell, because the owner *is* the business. Examples of this type include:

- A real estate brokerage firm with few to no agents

- An artist, author, or other craftsman, where the value of the business is linked to the creativity of the owner

- Travel agents with few to no employees who sometimes work out of their home

- An appraisal business working out of a home

- A small engineering firm consisting of the engineer and an administrative staff

- A building trade business, such as air conditioning and heating (HVAC), plumbing, or construction, where the owner works solo out of their house, using independent contractors as needed

- A licensed interior decorator working out of their home or a small shop with one to two employees or independent contractors
- The practices of licensed professions, such as doctors, chiropractors, dentists, and lawyers, which are dependent on relationships

In the above example, the decorator has skill sets that are not easily duplicated, so without the decorator, there is not much business. In some instances, however, decorators start their own businesses or buy one with several employees and a healthy customer base so the business is not dependent on a single person's talents, which would be more attractive to a buyer when being sold. Similarly, in a sole-practitioner medical practice, when the doctor leaves, the patients do too. So the ability to sell these businesses depends on their price and whether the owner is willing to stay on for one to five years to bridge the transition to the new owner. When an industry, such as HVAC, plumbing, real estate, or appraising, requires special skills or licenses, its practitioners are likely to start their own one-man or one-woman show or to buy an established business that has a location, employees, a customer base, FF&E, and—most important—positive cash flow.

SMALL BUSINESSES

Typical small businesses include cafés, coffee shops, small restaurants, bars, convenience stores, dry cleaners, clothing stores, gift shops, and day care centers. These enterprises typically have three to seven employees and are not 100 percent dependent on the owner working in the business to provide consumers with good service. However, the business is unlikely to succeed if the owner is not thoroughly involved in monitoring the quality of customer service, absenteeism, theft, and other important issues.

SMALL TO MEDIUM COMPANIES

Small to medium companies have about five to ten employees, typically grossing over $2 million annually, and include the distribution, manufacturing, wholesale, retail, education, medical, and service industries. The owner is usually involved in running the business, with a manager often running the day-to-day operations. These businesses are attractive to buyers looking for stable businesses—that is, companies that have employees in place and are making a profit.

MIDDLE-MARKET OR LARGER COMPANIES

Middle-market companies have been in business for years and have anywhere from fifteen to hundreds of employees, some of them tenured. Management structures are in place, so the owner may not be involved directly, and larger companies will typically have a CEO, CFO, and an operations manager. These companies have a significant client base and millions of dollars in annual revenues, making them quite desirable.

Every day, our company works with our database of thousands of buyers and private-equity firms, all looking for great businesses that operate on all six cylinders.

MENTORING CORNER

You have probably identified which kind of business you own from the categories listed in the chapter. However, you can always take demonstrative action to adjust your business to make it more attractive and to demand a higher price. Many times, a business will be built around the expertise or contacts of the founders. Ask yourself this: How are you able to leverage that expertise or those contacts so that the business is not dependent on the individual? The answer is establishing systems. A business that is system driven is much more attractive than one that is personality driven. You can also start involving a manager by delegating leadership authority and training him or her to replace you.

MISSION VERSUS CELEBRITY BUSINESS

It's important to ask new business owners to decide if they want to build a business around a mission brand or a celebrity brand at the very beginning of building their business. When a company name includes the name of the founder, it is most likely a business built as a celebrity brand. Tony Robbins is an example of a highly successful founder who created a celebrity-branded empire of companies, including Robbins Research International and Tony Robbins Productions. There are, of course, companies named after their founders that transcend the founders' names and become established brands, like famous fashion designers or companies like Mary Kay, Rolls-Royce, Mattel, Nordstrom, and Getty, just to name a few. And there are others that establish mission-based initiatives, such as the Rockefellers and Nobels.

When a business is built around a mission brand, it is much easier to create business systems to scale and eventually to sell than a business built around a person or their personality and notoriety. When selling a celebrity branded company, there will most likely be an ongoing commitment for the celebrity to stay involved at least for a transitional period.

 KNOW MORE TO EXIT RICH

When creating your exit strategy, it is important to know what type and size of business you have. This will help you target the right types of buyers. Equally important, you should determine if you have a business or a job to sell. If the former, you can work with your advisor to take steps to make your business more attractive to potential buyers. If, however, you have more of a job than a business, you will want to focus on strengthening your ST 6 P's which we will cover in part 2, before putting your company on the market.

DID YOU KNOW?

- There are 30.2 million businesses in the United States, and 99.9 percent are small businesses, according to the Office of Advocacy estimates. Small businesses employ about half of the US workforce.

- According to the Office of Advocacy, 20 percent of businesses fail in the first year.

- According to the Office of Advocacy, 641,759 businesses opened in 2010, and 813,353 closed in 2010. There were 56,282 bankruptcies in 2010, as well. More recently, 8,053 businesses closed in 2017, and 452,835 businesses started in 2014. There were also 796,037 bankruptcies filed for both business and personal accounts in 2017.

IMPLEMENTATION IS KEY

To further explore the lessons learned in this chapter, implement the following:

- Review your business model and figure out what type of business owner you are.

- Take the quiz: What Type of Business Do You Own? https://www.seilertuckeracademy.com/build-a-business/quiz.

- The one-man/one-woman-show businesses must duplicate themselves and create a business if they want to sell one day.

- The small business owner must start working on the business rather than in it. They must start duplicating themselves and creating processes that don't require the owner on a day-to-day basis.

- Align yourself with an expert who can help you grow an actual business rather than continuing to operate a job.

PART 2

THE ST 6 P METHOD®

4

The ST 6 P Method® and the Five Types of Buyers

"Ideas are easy. Implementation is hard."

—Guy Kawasaki

B ased on years of experience, Seiler Tucker has worked with all levels of businesses. We have learned that buyers will pay top dollar for businesses that operate on all six cylinders, or ST 6 P's. We have sold businesses that are barely hanging on. Even though you think your business doesn't have value, someone else may find value in it; as the old saying goes, "someone's junk is another man's treasure." We have sold businesses that have been around for decades, making huge profits. We have helped sellers through divorces, relocations, burnout, and bankruptcies, and we have helped sellers on their deathbeds. We have also worked with all types of buyers, from all walks of life. Because of this vast experience, we know what will sell, what won't sell, and most importantly, how to maximize our client's value.

It's imperative that you identify who your buyer will be and know their buying criteria. It's also imperative to know the different types of buyers. Most buyers look at a multitude of characteristics of the business they are interested in. Some buyers will purchase the business even if it does not function on all six cylinders, and others will not.

The ST 6 P's are the most important factors to consider when evaluating and preparing your business for sale. If your business is deficient in one or more of these areas, it's not functioning at full value and won't get its maximum price at sale. In the engine of your business, the ST 6 P's are the cylinders, because they *drive value*. Many businesses don't operate on all cylinders. Instead, they're sluggish, they waste fuel, and they break down. You can avoid this inefficiency by tuning up your business using the 6 P Method. If you follow this method, it'll take you wherever you want to go.

Following are the ST 6 P's that are needed to drive value to your business. Buyers will pay top dollar for businesses that operate on the ST 6 P's

THE ST 6 P METHOD®

01	**People** Do you have the right team?	
02	**Product** Does your product have a niche or intellectual property?	
03	**Process** Is your process efficient and/or proprietary?	

continued

04	**Proprietary** Do you have intellectual property (brands, patents, trademarks, databases, contracts in place, etc.)?	
05	**Patrons** Do you have a loyal client base who will go out of their way to purchase your products and services?	
06	**Profits** Are you operating at the highest profit margin for your specific industry?	

PEOPLE: DO YOU HAVE THE RIGHT PEOPLE WORKING IN YOUR BUSINESS?

Buyers are looking for a business, not a job. They don't want to buy your company and immediately have to start running it. For a buyer to consider a business to be sustainable, it must have the right people in place so they do not have to invest time and money into hiring and training employees to run their new company.

PRODUCT: DOES YOUR PRODUCT HAVE A NICHE?

Consider, for a moment, Blockbuster Video, which had a great product in its heyday but ran into the problem all companies face when they don't continually innovate and market: They die a slow death from consumers. Blockbuster watched Netflix become more powerful but did nothing to remain competitive. As a result, they became obsolete.

It's important to ask yourself if your industry or product is on the way up or on the way out. If it's on the way out, that doesn't mean you sell your company to some uneducated buyer; you innovate and market to make your business relevant and keep yourself out of bankruptcy. No buyer will buy a company that will be out of business in a couple of years, so make sure your company has a niche with staying power.

PROCESS: ARE YOUR BUSINESS PROCESSES EFFICIENT AND PRODUCTIVE?

Most people don't think about processes when selling a business, but processes are essential to a business and to building profits. A great product can't save a company that doesn't have systems to market that product, collect payments due, or schedule meetings with clients. Does your company constantly reinvent the wheel instead of having a standard system for running the day-to-day and long-term operations? Buyers want to know that the engine under the hood of your company runs efficiently and isn't held together with twine and baling wire.

PROPRIETARY: DO YOU HAVE INTELLECTUAL PROPERTY?

Anything that makes your company special or unique, such as patents, trademarks, and contracts in place, is proprietary and drives up the value of your business. You could even have proprietary assets you haven't thought of, like customer databases, which are often overlooked and undervalued. In 2014, the instant messaging service WhatsApp had over a billion users. Facebook paid $19 *billion* for it, because its database could be monetized. Buyers are looking for the edge, or competitive advantage, that sets your business apart from your competition or provides an opportunity to exploit.

PATRONS: IS YOUR CLIENT BASE DIVERSIFIED, OR DO YOU HAVE CUSTOMER CONCENTRATION?

A sustainable business is nimble and can pivot when necessary. A varied and diverse client base makes this possible. The 80/20 rule says that 80 percent of your revenue comes from just 20 percent of your clients. If that 20 percent all comes from the same sector and something happens to that sector, 80 percent of your revenue is at stake. You can always lose a single client and recover, but if most of your revenue depends on a single client or single category, you're tying your fortunes to the behavior of that industry, so make sure you have a diverse client base.

PROFITS: IS MONEY FLOWING IN AND OUT OF THE BUSINESS SO IT MAXIMIZES PROFITS?

If you're upside down in assets and inventory and your cash flow isn't providing the money you need to live on, you're *not* profitable. Why would a buyer be interested in a company that doesn't make money? Most buyers are not interested in buying a nonprofit. The only buyers interested in buying an unprofitable business are turnaround specialists and perhaps competitors or strategic buyers, especially if they can find a way to monetize any of the ST 6 P's. We have hundreds or thousands of buyers for highly profitable businesses. The higher the profits, the higher the multiple.

The one P that buyers will not pay for is potential. Many owners with struggling businesses say their company has potential. While buyers want a company with growth potential, they're not going to pay a premium for it, because they'll have to invest the time and money to possibly realize it.

Ask yourself how many P's are strong in your business and how many you still need to strengthen. Be honest. We find that many companies operate on typically two to three of the ST 6 P's. Few operate or continue to operate on all six. And even if they do operate on all six, it's not always the case; many things can happen to cause a business to lose footing from time to time and slip.

In the next several chapters, we will explore each of the ST 6 P's that buyers examine, as well as the questions buyers ask before they choose to look at a business. It's important to have the answers to the buyers' questions before putting your business on the market. Your answers to all these questions and more will dictate your business's selling price. Buyers will absolutely want to evaluate all of these characteristics of your business to determine if your business meets their buying criteria and is worthy of the price you are asking.

Therefore, it's important to strategically think and plan for all the intricate details that buyers will examine and review when evaluating your business. The more prepared you are to address buyers' objections up front, the better equipped you will be to handle these objections and obstacles when they occur.

To maximize value and determine what group of buyers is right for your business, you should consider engaging the assistance of a professional M&A or business brokerage firm. Experienced advisors and brokers will have a database of buyers sorted by the five types of buyers as well as have those buyers sorted based on their criteria, such as time frame, industry, location, price range, down payment, and EBITDA requirement. This is certainly something you should look into before hiring your advisor or broker.

THE FIVE TYPES OF BUYERS AND WHAT THEY WANT

You have your reasons for putting your business up for sale, and buyers have their reasons for buying it. Knowing who's more likely to buy your business can save you a lot of time and effort. Plus, it will aid in building your business to suit your specific type of buyer's buying criteria.

In this section, we're going to give you the rundown on the five types of buyers and share how to use their defining characteristics to your advantage. We can honestly call this *synthesized wisdom*, because it's the result and observation of a ton of experience, loads of conversations, and a bunch of successfully closed deals. Pay attention to this, because it will help you structure some of your business to appeal to a specific buyer. Strategy and planning lead to prosperity.

The 5 Types of Buyers

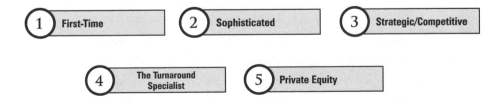

FIRST-TIME BUYERS

First-time buyers often want to get out of corporate America but earn the same amount of income, and hopefully more, by working for themselves. However, they don't know how to evaluate whether a business is operating on all six cylinders, or ST 6 P's, and they're often ignorant of the intricate details of buying a business; they may even look to use their retirement funds to make a tax-free down payment.

With their funds on the line, first-time buyers won't pull the trigger unless they feel safe and confident that they're making a good decision. They, instead, prefer to work with an advisor or business broker who can provide peace of mind by eliminating fears, protecting their interests, and helping them navigate the buying process.

SOPHISTICATED BUYERS

Sophisticated buyers have usually bought, started, and run their own businesses. They can tell when a business is making money and when a seller is trying to pull the wool over their eyes. They know what they want, so they're quick to pull the trigger. Sophisticated buyers also understand that M&A advisors and business brokers are the best way to find businesses that are properly vetted and meet their buying criteria.

COMPETITORS AND STRATEGIC BUYERS

Competitors and strategic buyers typically buy businesses that are in the same or a similar industry as the one they are already in. Strategic buyers will buy synergies in which to add additional profit centers, create congruent revenue streams, or solve a problem. Competitors and strategic buyers take advantage of the economy of scale; therefore, they valuate businesses differently than other buyers do. They look at how they can decrease overhead by streamlining operations and how they can better fulfill the demands of their existing clients. In addition, they acquire businesses to roll into their current portfolio in which to grow or sell their entire company for millions or billions of dollars. These buyers are sophisticated and know exactly what they are looking for. They, too, will solicit the assistance of M&A advisors or business brokers to help them locate businesses that meet their needs and buying criteria. Some of them buy 70 to 80 percent of a business, leaving 20 to 30 percent of the ownership with the previous owner to keep him or her there.

PRIVATE EQUITY BUYERS

Private equity buyers have funding in place or disposable income, so they move fast. They'll look at quite a few deals before they find one that matches their criteria, and most won't buy a business that doesn't have a management team in place.

PEGs (private equity groups) include opportunistic investors who review many deals looking for businesses that need recapitalization, leverage build-ups, management buyouts, or innovation and buy based on two strategies:

They buy based on the platform, or the desire to enter a new industry. If a PEG wants to build a food-manufacturing portfolio, for example, and they are not currently in that space, they will search for food manufacturing companies producing EBITDAs of at least $2 million and up.

Or they buy based on an add-on. PEGs acquire strategic businesses to add to their current portfolio within a field or industry where they already have a platform established. Their requirements for add-ons are less than their requirements for platforms, because they don't need as much EBITDA because of the strength of their current platform. PEGs continually send M&A or business brokerage firms a list of industries and their criteria.

Professional M&A advisors and business brokerage firms will sort these PEGs by their requirements: interest (platform or add-ons), industry, location, and EBITDA range. This is the most effective way to match sellers with private equity buyers. We currently work with thousands of private equity firms.

TURNAROUND SPECIALISTS

Turnaround specialists search for businesses that are doing poorly and that others overlook and undervalue. They fix what's wrong and transform them into profit-generating businesses. They often sell the renovated company. While they have many methods for finding makeover candidates, they often hire an M&A advisor or business broker, who brings them businesses they couldn't find on their own.

All five types of buyers have their own unique systems to evaluate the company's operation to see if the business drives on all ST 6 P's, as outlined here. Ask yourself which buyer will be best suited to purchase your business. Your answer will depend on how many cylinders you're currently operating on. At Seiler Tucker, the 6 P Method is one of the main topics we're asked to discuss in all the interviews we do.

MENTORING CORNER

Being an expert in your field means you most likely already know who some of your potential buyers may be.

- It may be a competitor in your area that wants a greater market share.

- It may be a competitor in a different location that wants to move into your territory.

- It may be a business in a related industry that wants to expand their business into your industry.

In reviewing potential buyers, you should also consider whether they are interested in your ongoing operations (and therefore keeping your business operating after the sale and therefore retaining most of your employees) or whether they may want to absorb your operations into their own. For instance, a local competitor may want to absorb your operations, while a competitor from out of state would want to keep your business operating, therefore creating a footprint for them in your market.

Understanding the goals of any potential buyers can also help you present your business in the best light. Sophisticated buyers look for a synergistic value-add—or some resource that the business they are looking at needs—that the buyer can supply that will multiply (or at least significantly increase) the valuation of the company after they purchase it. The synergistic value-add is often capital, but sometimes manufacturing capacity, distribution channels, and know-how are considered if they would facilitate more efficient or more cost-effective operations. Knowing the buyer's intentions will allow you to emphasize the advantages your business will provide them.

Knowing your potential buyer's intentions may also indicate whether they want to buy your business outright (stock purchase or entity purchase) or whether they want to simply buy the assets of your business (asset purchase, where you will still own the entity and therefore still owe any liabilities and debts of the business). If you need to pay off liabilities and debts, you will need a higher price to net the same profit from selling your stock or entity outright.

In preparing to address the ST 6 P's as outlined in the rest of this book, you may want to start by asking yourself if you have built your business on a solid foundation. When working with business owners, it's important to share the importance of every aspect of building a business that is sustainable, scalable, and ultimately salable by introducing the Essential Components of a Successful Business.

THE ESSENTIAL COMPONENTS OF A SUCCESSFUL BUSINESS

Review your own business as it relates to each of the areas in the image below to get you ready to implement the ST 6 P's. The outer ring of the image includes your overall mission, which defines the problem you want to solve or the need that you want to serve. As the leadership representative, you and your team are charged with holding the overall strategy and direction of your business to fulfilling the company's mission.

Within the circle, you will find the essential aspects that are needed to deliver on the mission of your business.

continued

Legal

First off, you will want to know if you have the right legal foundation for your business. From entity selection to tight legal agreements with all parties involved in your business operations, make sure you have identified your intellectual property, protected it, and then leveraged it.

Available Resources

Next, you will want to make sure you have sufficient funding to continue building your business. Ask yourself whether your cash flow allows you to grow. If not, check in to make sure you are making use of other people's money, other people's time, and other people's resources.

Relationships

The relationships with your customers, suppliers, employees, and investors are all crucial to helping you fulfill your company's mission. You will want to make sure you have the right systems in place to nurture and grow these relationships.

Communications and Marketing

You will also want to look at your communications and marketing efforts. Do you have ongoing communication processes that create your customer journey, establishing a lifetime relationship with your customers? Make sure your lead magnet marketing and sales funnels are working and that you have a system to analyze them and adjust them regularly.

Business Systems

These are the lifeblood of any business and create the difference between owning a business and owning a job. Your business systems can be your competitive advantage. From how the phone is answered to how customer service issues are handled, every step of your business processes should be documented to provide clarity and consistency.

Deliverable

Your product or service is your deliverable. Your deliverable is the reason behind creating your business and can be most successful if every other aspect of your business described in the Essential Components of a Successful Business is established and operational.

After you have analyzed your business using the Essential Components of a Successful Business, you have most likely identified additional areas that can increase your value to a potential buyer, as well as highlighting your competitive advantage over other companies in your field.

Packaging Your Business

The next few chapters will provide an in-depth look at the Seiler Tucker 6 P Method. This system will help you package your business for potential buyers.

Where the Essential Components of a Successful Business show you how to *build* a successful business, the ST 6 P's will show you how to successfully *sell* your business. While the purpose for developing them may be different, the information and guidance in them is much the same:

ST 6 P's	ESSENTIAL COMPONENTS OF A SUCCESSFUL BUSINESS
People	**Leadership, team, relationships**
Product	**Deliverable**
Process	**Business systems, communications, marketing**
Proprietary	**Mission, legal, business systems, deliverable**
Patrons	**Customers, clients**
Profits	**Available resources**

By following the advice and strategies outlined here, you will be preparing your business to attract the best buyers, perform well through the due diligence process, and garner the highest price when it comes time to sell.

GOLDEN NUGGET

5

 **People**

*"You don't build a business—you build people
—then people build the business."*

—Zig Ziglar

Thus far, we have discussed the type of business you own, the different types of buyers, and their buying criteria. In the chapters ahead, we will dig into each one of the ST 6 P's to further illustrate what buyers are looking for and how you should measure and tune up each of the ST 6 P's in your business.

Most buyers do not want to buy a job; they want to buy a business with tenured employees who will be committed and loyal to the new owner. Buyers want to buy a business that works for them, not one where they will have to work for it. Therefore, the number-one factor to a buyer is people, which is the first P.

Business owners always tell us that they own a business, not a job, and they truly believe it. Therefore, we start asking business owners a series of questions to test their perception and help them determine if they own a job or a business.

THE WHO OF YOUR BUSINESS

Every business has responsibilities that must be handled by a management team or employee and preferably not the owner. Therefore, it's imperative that you list out all the decision-making tasks, no matter how big or small, and then write the position title next to that seat. In this section, we will review a list of responsibilities that may exist in your business. The WHO in this instance is the department that handles those decisions. The goal is that the owner does not put their name next to any of these items, because it's imperative that the business not be reliant on the founder. If it is, then the business will not be scalable, and most buyers will not be attracted to buy it. As we always say, "If you don't have an assistant, then you are the assistant."

The following questions will help you determine your WHO and shed some light on where you need to strengthen your first P:

- Who opens and closes the business?
- Who handles or oversees sales?
- Who has the client relationships?
- Who handles customer service?
- Who handles product development?
- Who handles the marketing?
- Who is in charge of CAC (customer acquisition cost)?
- Who makes bank deposits?
- Who does the alarm company contact when there is an emergency?
- Who handles problems and puts out fires in regard to the following?
    - Employee issues
    - Client issues
    - Product issues
    - Service issues

- o Equipment issues

- o Environmental issues

- o Operational issues

- o Accounting issues

- o Banking issues

- o Legal issues

- o Software issues

- o Union issues

- Who determines employee hours?

- Who addresses employees when they don't show up?

- Who determines vacation schedules?

- How long can you be away from your business and your business will still run smoothly?

- Who runs the business?

- Who engages in the day-to-day activities of your business?

- Who reports the KPIs (key performance indicators)?

- Who is on call when there is an emergency?

You will also want to assess how often you take vacations and whether your business can run smoothly if you are away for more than a few days at a time. If you are unable to take time away from your work and if the answer to the WHO in most of the questions above is you, you own a job, not a business.

TEAMWORK MAKES THE DREAM WORK

Without people, there is no business. Therefore, every buyer's number-one question and concern is the WHO. The WHO are the employees and management team that must be in place to perform all the functions to cover as many seats as possible for the business to run smoothly and, most importantly, without the owner.

Let's look at some examples of seats in a company and the WHO that is needed to operate the seats. One employee can operate multiple seats. The key is to have enough tenured employees and management team members to operate all of the seats. The business owner should be the visionary, not the implementer. In other words, the owners should work *on* the business not *in* it.

EXAMPLE OF SEATS IN A COMPANY

- Answering the phones, transferring calls, taking messages
- Checking and ordering supplies
- Dealing with vendors
- Greeting clients
- Cleaning up
- Checking and opening mail
- Data entry
- Banking
- Invoicing
- Accounts receivables
- Accounts payables
- Controlling overhead
- Inventory control
- Maintaining equipment and vehicles
- Maintaining leases and/or real estate property
- KPIs
- Recruitment
- Hiring and firing
- Training employees
- Employee meetings
- Human resource issues
- Marketing
- New product development

- Sales

- Operations, policies, and procedures

- Training employees

- Customer service

- Client agreements

- Handling bids

- Quality control

- IT

- Software

- Internet compliance

- Environmental issues

- Negotiating leases and/or obtaining real estate appraisals

KNOWING WHO OVERSEES THE SEATS

We have just identified many seats in a company. However, depending on the business, there can be a lot more seats that have to be assigned to an employee or a management team. Almost every business owner's number-one concern is the employees. In fact, they are what keeps business owners up at night, and, in some cases, they are what inspires them to sell. As we mentioned before, there is no business without employees. Without employees, all you have is a glorified job, so it is important to answer the next question: Who oversees the seats?

The lack of employees and a management team is the number-one reason businesses don't sell. I could use countless stories to illustrate that point. In fact, I have so many stories that I could write a book titled *Buyers Want to Buy a Business, Not a Job!* In the next few sections, I will share a few examples to illustrate the importance of having the right employees and management team in place.

MANUFACTURING AND DISTRIBUTION BUSINESS

We once tried selling a multimillion-dollar distribution and manufacturing company that had been in business for decades. This business was well established and had weathered all sorts of financial storms. They had a great product and loyal client base. However, what they did not have were loyal employees. The owner had hired his sister as the office manager, and he relied on her to run his entire company. The big problem with this company was that they had no tenured employees. Most employees had been there under a year, and all the company's data was in the owner's head. This is a buyer's worst nightmare, because if anything should happen to the owner, they would be out of business, and their entire investment could disappear.

We coached this client on the importance of building a staff and a strong management team. We went as far as connecting the owner and his sister with a recruiter. However, as the saying goes, you can lead a horse to water, but you can't make him drink. After trying for several years to work with this client, we were not able to sell their company.

It's now been several years, and they still have the same issues: no tenured employees and no management team. The owner is up in age and will not be able to continue working at the same pace. Unfortunately, since they did not listen and try to do things differently by building a sellable business for a proper exit, they will most likely end up going out of business, and their nest egg won't be golden.

MACHINE AND FABRICATION BUSINESS

We are currently working with a machine and fabrication company that has been in business over thirty years. Their unique selling proposition is that they can make and weld anything for anyone. They are completely customized and create on demand. This is a great company with a sustainable service, and they have a loyal, diversified customer base that has been with them for decades. Additionally, their financials are sound, with a healthy profit margin.

Their business will be attractive to many buyers, except for one thing: their lack of employees. The company is owned by two equal partners who work in the business, and they have only two employees in the shop. These employees don't interact with the clients, nor do they know or understand anything about operating the business. The bigger issues are that all the intellectual property is in the owners' heads; therefore, if the owners leave, the clients leave! Again, this is a great business that operates on most of the ST 6 P's, except they don't have tenured employees and a management team in place.

We have educated the sellers, stating that they must stay on for two to three years to share their knowledge with the new owners. However, because the owners must stay on for two to three years, we will not be able to add back their entire salary and benefits, because they are not willing to work for free and will expect to get paid (the same or lower compensation) with owner's benefits. This lowers the company's EBITDA (earnings before interest, taxes, depreciation, and amortization), which will ultimately lower the sales price of the business.

Unfortunately, stories like these are prevalent, and there are more businesses without tenured, loyal employees than there are businesses with them. It does not mean that we can't sell your business without employees in place, but it certainly makes it much more difficult to do so and much harder to maximize the value.

BUYERS' QUESTIONS

Buyers will ask a series of questions to determine if the business has a loyal tenured staff. And if they don't actually ask these questions, we can assure you that they are thinking of them. These questions include:

- How many employees do you have?
- What is their skill level?
- What is your employee retention rate?
- What is your average employee tenure?
- Is it difficult to find skilled employees for your industry?
- How many employees do you replace per year?
- What employee agreements do you have in place?
- Do you have any noncompete agreements with your employees?
- What is the average compensation plan and employee benefit program that you offer?
- What is your recruitment method?
- How much money do you spend on training per year?
- Do you have an in-house human resource department?
- Can your business run without you?
- Do you have a management team in place, and will they assist with the transfer?

- Do you have a COO (chief operation officer) or general manager?
- Do you have a CFO (chief financial officer) or an in-house bookkeeper?

EMPLOYEE DOCUMENTS

In addition to the standard buyers' questions, all buyers will want to review a series of documents prior to purchasing your business. These documents include the following:

- Organizational chart
- Employee handbook
- Policies and procedures manual
- Employee agreements (nondisclosure and assignment of intellectual property clauses)
- Noncompete agreements
- Employee benefit programs

You might be reading this and saying, "I don't have any of these documents!" It's okay; many business owners don't have them before reading this book. Remember: It's never too late to start drafting your employee documents. The more organized your employee records are, the more a buyer will be comfortable in purchasing your business. Believe it or not, even large companies are not as prepared as they should be when it comes to their employees' documentation.

For example, we sold a manufacturing company for millions. They had over fifty employees. The buyer kept requesting the employee handbooks, agreements, and noncompete agreements. The seller kept saying they would produce them during due diligence. However, during due diligence, their company's in-house CPA could not find these documents. Therefore, before and during the closing, I went to each employee and had them sign new employee agreements and noncompete agreements. This could have become a huge issue, because employees don't have to agree to sign new agreements, especially if they are not being compensated to do so. If they had refused, the entire deal would have fallen apart. Luckily, I was able to obtain all the signatures.

EXAMPLE ORGANIZATIONAL CHART

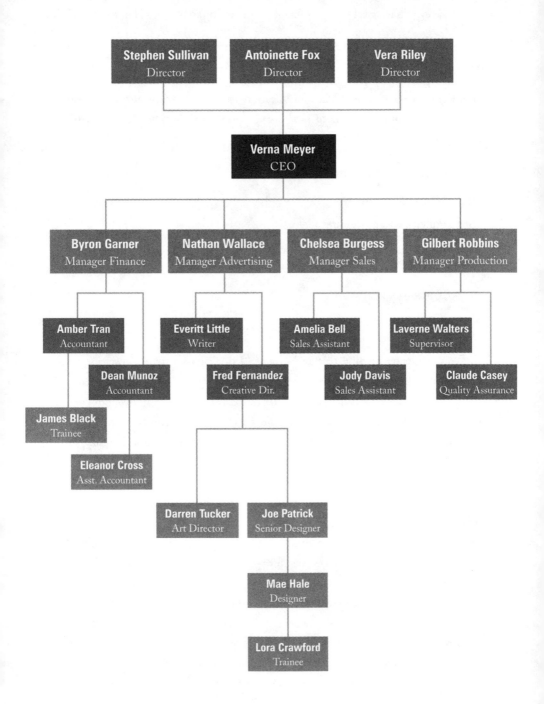

THE BUYER'S BIG QUESTION AND CONCERN

Now, while you aren't willing to wait years for your business to sell, you need to know that a final sale may depend on your availability. You need to know that the buyer's big question and concern will be how long it will take to train the new owner in this industry or business.

An experienced buyer knows that future success depends on how long the seller is willing to stay on to train the new owner. This training is *always* included in the sale of a business to ensure a smooth transition. Depending on the size of your business (and how well you've managed the people and processes components of the ST 6 P's), the industry, and the skills and experience of the buyer, you might expect to stay on for a week or up to five years.

While training is included in the sale, the seller's time doesn't have to be, if the sale is negotiated properly. Some industries and businesses can take weeks, months, and even years to properly train the buyer. Most small businesses require only one to four weeks of training. Medium-size businesses usually require two to four months. Larger businesses may require the owner to stay on with pay for one to five years.

Having the right employees and management team can make or break the sale of your company. In the following example, you will see just how beneficial this was for the seller.

For more than twenty years, a multimillion-dollar dental lab with a staff of seven technicians and administrators produced crowns and veneers. Doctors sent business to the owner, who had built strong relationships with dentists over the past two decades. This was a sought-after company in a strong industry, and when the owner was ready to sell, we found a qualified and motivated buyer with years of sales experience in the dental community. However, the buyer had no experience in the company's line of work and felt the only way it could work was if the seller agreed to stay on for five years so the business wouldn't suffer.

We structured a deal where the buyer paid the seller $100,000 a year for working full time for the first year and part time for the next four. If the seller helped the buyer increase revenue and control costs, he'd also share in those profits. The buyer was willing to negotiate these generous terms because the company was strong in an industry that was on the way up. The seller was equally delighted to earn at least a half-million dollars extra that he hadn't counted into his asking price.

This is a great example of a win-win scenario and the importance of people in negotiating a sale. The other P's can play critical roles too, in ways that illustrate the importance of not waiting too long to make improvements in how the business runs before you plan to sell.

MENTORING CORNER

The people or human aspect of your business is critically important. Often, the reputation of the founder or the company's management team may be what attracts a potential buyer. In this case, the buyer will want to make sure they are retained after the sale.

On the other hand, a buyer may only be interested in the nonhuman assets or aspects of your business. In this case, as a seller, you may want to address how you will take care of your team as part of the sale. For instance, you can require the buyer to add severance packages for your management team and employees over and above the purchase price of your business.

PRESERVING YOUR EXPERTISE AND KNOW-HOW

Your business depends on your expertise and know-how, and this may be very specialized. However, this expertise may make it difficult or too expensive to hire an employee with your same level of expertise if, in fact, any exist. If you don't want to have to stay with the business forever, it's important to develop the processes that include training and implementing your expertise and know-how that can be successfully applied by less specialized and knowledgeable employees. This leverages your ability and allows for expansion and your eventual replacement.

This may also apply to the expertise and know-how of essential employees within your business. Procedure manuals that reach the most detailed level of operations, particularly technical and manufacturing operations, are one of the best protections against loss of necessary know-how if an employee leaves your business.

HOW TO KEEP ESSENTIAL EMPLOYEES THROUGH THE SALES PROCESS

When you are in the process of selling, retaining essential employees is important for maintaining the highest valuation of your company. When employees hear that you may be selling, panic for their own future may negatively affect their performance or cause them to start exiting. The following can help protect against employees leaving:

- Offer employment contracts, often called "golden handcuffs," which specify certain financial incentives that are meant to encourage employees to remain with a company for a certain period of time.

- Offer a "golden parachute," which is an agreement with the employee (usually an executive) in which the employee will receive certain significant benefits if their employment is terminated.

- Require noncompete and nonsolicitation agreements that are properly written and can be enforced in many jurisdictions.

- Offer confidentiality agreements that include a provision preventing employees from taking positions where they are inevitably likely to call on confidential information of the company.

Remember that your people help create the success of your business and can be an extremely important part of selling it. When Sharon sold the talking book business, for example, the buyer intended to only retain a few management people for a short time while they incorporated the operations of the company into theirs. As part of the sales negotiations, they were able to secure severance packages for all the employees who stayed through the date of sale (based on their tenure with the company), and they also brought in an outplacement firm to help them find new employment opportunities.

 **KNOW MORE TO EXIT RICH**

In this chapter, we covered the first P, people. As you learned, buyers do not want to buy a job. They want to buy a business with committed employees who can continue to keep it running profitably for them after the sale. Take steps now to ensure that you have the right people in place to build a business that is running strongly and is scalable. You'll be glad you did at the closing table.

DID YOU KNOW?

- According to Compdata Surveys, the average employee turnover rate is 18.5 percent.
- One-third of surveyed owners had not even thought about management succession, and only 25 percent were comfortable that their managerial team would be successful if the owner wasn't involved after the transition.
- According to the National Association for the Self-Employed, 79.66 percent of small businesses are self-employed individuals.

IMPLEMENTATION IS KEY

To further explore the lessons learned in this chapter, implement the following:

- Know the WHO in your company.
- Review the seats and assign a team member to each seat.

Create the following employee documents:

- Organizational chart
- Employee handbook

- Employee agreements, noncompete agreements, obligation of confidentiality, or assignment of intellectual property
- Policy and procedure manuals
- Training manuals

To enjoy free access to additional employee documents, please visit SeilerTuckerAcademy.com.

6

 # Product

> *"Business has only two functions:*
> *marketing and innovation."*
> **—Milan Kundera**

The second P to consider is product. When looking at your business, ask yourself whether your product or service is on the way up or on the way out. In other words, are you the next Blockbuster Video to be pushed out by Netflix, or are you the next Netflix that is pushing out your competitors? This P is very important and never overlooked by buyers. Buyers are fearful of investing in a company that will quickly become obsolete.

The number-one thing we always tell our clients is to ABM and ABI (always be marketing and always be innovating). It's imperative to know your competition, know the trends, and to always be ahead of the curve. In fact, not only is it important to know your competition; it's also just as crucial to study other industry leaders. At Seiler Tucker, we've studied industry leaders such as Disney World, The Ritz-Carlton, Zappos, Apple, Google, Facebook, and WeWork. These brands are the leaders of this century, and many have been around for decades. They are well known for their marketing and innovation efforts, and they continue to reinvent themselves to stay current and appeal to new generations. You can always gain great insight and wisdom to improve your business and learn new ways to market and innovate.

However, the companies that become complacent will be left behind, like Blockbuster. In fact, Blockbuster saw the writing on the wall with Netflix. Unfortunately, Blockbuster was fat and happy; they never thought they would be dethroned. Boy, were they wrong.

Some other companies that got it all wrong were Kodak, Blackberry, IBM, Toys "R" Us, and Kmart. These companies are legendary and thought they would weather all storms; however, they did not weather the "branding" storm. These brands did not plan, market, and innovate for new consumers, such as millennials. You have heard the saying, "You're only as good as your last sale!" The same holds true for brands: You're only as good as your competitors if you continue to market and innovate.

TOP INDUSTRIES ON THE DECLINE

Ask yourself again: Is your industry on the way up or on the way out? This is an important question for all sellers to ponder. Many industries are practically a dying breed. According to *The Wall Street Journal, Forbes, Inc., USA Today*, and MSN, the following industries are unlikely to ever fully bounce back from the recession:

- Office supplies
- Bookstores
- Security
- Commodity exchanges
- Sound recording studios
- Textile and fabric finishing mills

- Curtain and linen mills
- Saving institutions
- Formal wear
- Costume rental
- Port and harbor operations
- Online mortgage brokers
- Tank and armored vehicle manufacturing
- Wired telecommunications carriers
- Newspaper publishing
- Apparel manufacturing
- DVD, game, and video rentals
- Manufactured home dealers
- Video postproduction services
- Photofinishing

INDUSTRIES ON THE CUTTING EDGE

However, there are many industries that are thriving and on the cutting edge. Look over the following list to see if yours made the cut:

- VoIP providers
- Wind power
- E-commerce and online auctions
- Environmental consulting
- Biotechnology
- Tech and gaming
- Solar power
- Third-party administrators and insurance claims adjusters
- Correctional facilities

- Internet publishing
- Peer-to-peer lending platforms
- Cider production
- Telehealth services
- Motion capture software development
- Computer systems design and related services
- Contractors (building finishing, foundation, structure, building interior, building equipment, specialty trade)
- Construction (residential building, nonresidential building, heavy and civil engineering)
- Drone technology
- Broadcasting

CAN YOUR BUSINESS BE DUPLICATED OR FRANCHISED?

Now ask yourself this: Is your business something extremely unique, with little competition that you can duplicate or franchise? If so, you could be well positioned to turn your business into a revenue-generating franchise.

At Seiler Tucker, we have worked with a multitude of business owners who wanted to sell their business simply because the challenge was gone. They had done everything they felt they could possibly do to grow their business to the next level. They wanted to sell so they could take the revenues and go create their next masterpiece.

When we sit down with our clients, we look at all their reasons for selling, the problems they are experiencing, the options we can explore to create their exit strategy, and how we can solve their immediate problems. We evaluate a seller's business and their concerns, along with their need for change, even if it is complete boredom.

In turn, we can either sell our client's business or assist them with franchise development. If a seller is bored and lacks a challenge, for example, but they still like what they do and still believe in their products and services, we can help them create a franchise system and grow their company using other people's money. This opens a whole new world of possibilities. Not only is the seller continuing their legacy and helping their clients, but they are also providing an opportunity for other individuals to own a piece of the American dream. These individuals will flourish in the business the seller first created.

HOW MANY REVENUE STREAMS DO YOU HAVE?

When a company has multiple sources of income and multiple profit centers, that company becomes much more attractive to buyers. Many businesses go out of business every year because all their eggs were in one basket.

We are working with several publishing companies that have been in business for years. Most are lifestyle-oriented magazines that are looking to sell. Their net worth ranges between a quarter of a million dollars and six million. All are quite profitable and function on most of the ST 6 P's. However, the one P that they are missing is product.

Many publishing companies are going out of business because most print is becoming obsolete as digital becomes the preferred delivery method for content and as the demand for hard copy printed publications rapidly decreases. We coach our clients into creating congruent revenue streams by adding a digital platform. If they don't do this, they will not be able to sell their company for maximum value.

Buyers will still purchase a publishing company; however, if it is strictly print, they will deeply discount the cash flow so they can earmark the funds for adding a digital component to the publication after the sale so they are able to stay relevant in the eyes of the consumer.

WHAT SPECIAL SKILL SETS AND LICENSES ARE NEEDED IN YOUR PARTICULAR BUSINESS OR INDUSTRY?

Every industry is different, requiring a different set of skills. The skills and licenses are not as important as long as you have employees and managers in place. Most first-time buyers tend to purchase a business that they believe is easy to own and operate. Make no mistake about it: There is no such thing as a business that is easy to own and operate. Owning and operating your own business is hard work. That is why many businesses fail in the first five years. First-time buyers gravitate toward coffee shops, cafés, restaurants, bars,

Laundromats, convenience stores, and day care centers. These are not easy businesses to operate; however, they are easier than many businesses requiring specialized skill sets and training.

Technical businesses requiring specialized skill sets and licenses are more difficult to sell. The reason for this is they are more difficult to find qualified buyers for and more difficult to obtain lending for, because lenders want buyers to have industry experience. It is difficult for a buyer to buy an air conditioning and heating company, for example, if they are not experienced and licensed in the trade. The company may have employees in place, but what happens if the employees walk out of the business? Then the owner will be in a pickle. Because of this, some industries require special licenses that the buyer must obtain before he or she closes on the business.

FASTEST GROWING INDUSTRIES IN THE UNITED STATES

According to *Forbes*, the following nine industries are heating up:

- Heavy and civil engineering construction
- Beverage manufacturing
- Personal services
- Direct selling establishments
- Building finishing contractors
- Real estate
- Durable goods
- Specialized freight trucking
- Architectural, engineering, and related services

MENTORING CORNER

There is no doubt that innovation is key to maintaining and growing a successful business. A buyer will be looking at the life cycle of the products

continued

and services of your business, as well as trends in your industry, to assess whether you are in tune with them.

REVIEW YOUR ASSETS

As an example, when we see a large inventory balance on a company's balance sheet, we immediately want to know why. If the company is preparing for a new product launch and is getting the inventory ready for it, that is a good explanation. If, however, the inventory turn cycle has lengthened and the inventory is becoming obsolete or less desirable when compared to a competitor's, that is not good.

During the due diligence process, a buyer will review all of your assets on the balance sheet of your business to assess current salability, as well as current market value. You will need to be prepared to validate all of your assets prior to the sale, so take steps now to ready yourself for this process.

STAYING IN TUNE WITH TECHNOLOGY

The examples given in this chapter of the dramatic impact and changes in the publishing industry and the brick-and-mortar retail stores are spot on in that they did not foresee and innovate to capitalize on the impact of the Internet both for e-commerce and for product delivery. As such, they were overrun by more agile and innovative alternatives. Therefore, it's important when selling to identify both your strengths and your weaknesses in these areas and to be prepared to address them during due diligence.

 KNOW MORE TO EXIT RICH

In this chapter, you got to meet the second P, product. When evaluating your business for sale, determine whether your product or service is on the way up or on the way out. Taking steps to ensure your product is relevant and on the cutting edge will make your business more desirable to buyers and help you get a higher price for your business when you are ready to sell.

DID YOU KNOW?

- According to *The New York Times*, by rethinking the business model surrounding shaving, Dollar Shave Club now has 3.2 million members and was recently acquired by Unilever for a reported $1 billion.

- Reenvisioning the business model for driving through its subscription service, Zipcar allows members to rent a nearby car by the day or by the hour. This is a radical shift away from the existing car ownership and car rental business models.

- According to a 2019 *Forbes* article, there are seven industries that will be disrupted in the next ten years: financial services (particularly investing), health care, fashion clothing, insurance, legal services, the moving industry, and home furnishings.

IMPLEMENTATION IS KEY

To further explore the lessons learned in this chapter, implement the following:

- If your industry is dying, think of congruent revenue streams and add them to your business.

- Acquire a smaller strategic or complementary type of business.

- Evaluate your competition, and see what they are doing to stay relevant.

- Evaluate your consumer base, and see what you can do to stay current and relevant so you can continue to gain market share.

- Explore ways that you can add additional profit centers to your business.

To enjoy a free video of Michelle discussing her personal experiences, case studies, and how you can put these lessons into practice for your business, please visit SeilerTuckerAcademy.com.

Process

"Perfection has to do with the end product,
but excellence has to do with the process."
—Jerry Moran

T his third P is typically overlooked and gets less attention than most of the other ST 6 P's. However, process is huge and should not be neglected when trying to build and sell your business. Process can truly make or break your company, because it can influence how profitably and efficiently a business operates.

Your process should be carefully thought out and should take into consideration every touch point of your business. Processes should be efficient and consistent. They should start and end with the customer experience in mind. If you are able to get this part right, your business will grow exponentially.

Most business owners, however, never consider the customer experience in their process building. This is unfortunate, because when the process is efficient and productive, it leads to great customer service and satisfaction. In this chapter, we're going to look at some great examples of how a well-thought-out and implemented process enhances the customer experience. As we're looking at some of the most successful chains in America, ask yourself what makes their processes work.

When you think of McDonald's, "systematic" probably comes to mind. They have a well-defined, well-oiled, systematic process that is consistent across their franchises. Any employee can come in and easily start working after reading and training on the McDonald's systems. You can also walk into any McDonald's franchise anywhere in the world and know what to expect. For example, you know that the classic McDonald's french fries in Paris are going to taste exactly like they do at the McDonald's in your hometown.

Despite some employee glitches from time to time, the customer experience is the same. Their unique selling proposition is consistency. Love or hate their food, they are the most well-branded fast food chain because of their consistent processes.

In fact, you should watch *The Founder*. In this movie, the McDonald brothers spent hours upon hours role-playing in an empty field, practicing who takes the order, heats the buns, cooks the burgers, puts the pickles on, etc. This movie was based on the process development that took place over sixty years ago. Processes are not new; the idea has been in effect for decades. The issue is that, because most business owners are so busy working in their business rather than on their business, they have neglected creating, documenting, implementing, and training on processes.

Like McDonald's, Burger King's processes are systematic. You know when you go to any Burger King in the world that you're going to have the same experience. You're going to have it your way. Big brands like these two could not grow worldwide if they did not have a consistent process in place that enhances the customer experiences.

There are also major conglomerates that have bad processes in place. These processes should be replaced immediately, as they diminish the customer experience and, in some cases, infuriate clients. We come across a lack of process all the time when dealing with business owners.

One time, we were working with a candle manufacturing company that had applied to be on the hit show *The Profit* on CNBC. This company operated on a few of the ST 6 P's. Their biggest issue, however, was process: They had none. They had few employees filling many seats. To make matters worse, these employees were overworked, underpaid, and underappreciated.

According to the seller, their business was accepted to film on the show but then was rejected, because the seller breached the network's agreement. The owner reached out to us to either sell or partner with their business. We toured the facility and met with the employees. We were shocked by the lack of leadership and by processes that were never established for a company that had been in existence for decades. As we walked into the manufacturing plant, we noticed there were no machines, no processes, and no flow. We saw employees who were making the candles by hand, one by one. Their product was in demand and unique; however, their business was not sustainable, because they could only make one candle at a time.

We discovered they were turning down orders because of the lack of real manufacturing equipment and the lack of processes and employees to handle the workload. They had way too many SKUs that were not moving; however, they would interrupt the assembly line to make a few candles at a customer's request. There was no rhyme or reason to their process.

We soon discovered that the combined plant and warehouse was a complete disaster. There was no real inventory system, and the owner's kids took inventory whenever they wanted so they could sell the product on the street and put money in their pocket. We noticed that the packaging was unappealing and that there was no real customer service.

Additionally, money flew out the door, as the owner and children took money out of the business whenever they felt like it. The staff's pay was low, considering the number of years they had worked there and the work they were doing. The owner never came in during the day; however, the owner would call the staff at all hours of the night with unreasonable demands. The owner would also yell and berate the employees daily. The owner also had retail stores under the same corporate name as the company.

It came as no surprise to learn that the financials were a nightmare. This company was one of the worst run businesses we had ever seen. It was a shame, because they functioned on most of the ST 6 P's: They had a great product, dedicated employees, loyal clients, and were well branded. But they had no process and, because of that, no profits.

We could have turned this business around and sold it for maximum value to one of our existing buyers. However, the business owner was not a willing participant, refusing to listen and implement change. This owner was so defiant, unprofessional, and disrespectful to their staff that we ended up walking away.

We saw that the staff was pleasant and dedicated and that they had great ideas for streamlining and creating processes. They wanted change, but the owner was unwilling. We would have bought this business ourselves if we could have gotten rid of the owner. In most cases, it's the owner that's the issue, not the employees. I'm sure you are familiar with the expression "the fish stinks from the head." If the problem comes from the top and the person is unwilling to accept your help, the best thing you can do is walk away. We share this because buyers want to make sure a business has processes that are streamlined and well documented, in the form of flowcharts and policy and procedure manuals. They also want to ensure that the employees are trained and compliant on these processes. And if these are nonexistent and the owner is unwilling to change, there is not much you can do to encourage a good sale.

MENTORING CORNER

Just as our body cannot operate without our respiratory system or our heart pumping blood, a business can only operate through its own systems. If those systems are well thought out and documented, the business can both sustain its success and scale larger more quickly. However, if the system is one of chaos and indecision, the business is destined for failure.

Business systems help define best practices for creating success in your business, through design, sourcing, production, marketing, distribution, collections, and customer service. These systems also provide consistency, quality control, and assessment. Each one of these steps should be documented and fine-tuned as improvements are made. In fact, that fine-tuning process may create additional intellectual property that can provide more of a competitive advantage for your business.

continued

MANAGE TO SYSTEMS

One of the greatest benefits of having good business systems becomes apparent in the management of your employees. It is much easier to manage to a system than it is to manage to a personality. Managing to a system helps take the emotion out of managing employees. For instance, one of my clients had a problem dealing with her millennial receptionist. Even though she has a documented code of conduct that the employee was violating, she was trying to talk to the employee about her behavior, which was not being received well. I suggested she adjust her approach to asking the employee to review the code of conduct for the business and share which ones she was violating. The conversation became much more productive, even generating some shared laughter, and the situation was resolved.

Your business systems will generally create great off-balance-sheet value for your business. As such, it is important to document your systems through operational manuals, policy and procedure manuals, and flowcharts. In addition, be careful about how much you reveal to potential buyers without the protection of a confidentiality agreement. It is important to protect this valuable competitive advantage.

 KNOW MORE TO EXIT RICH

In this chapter, we learned about the third P, process. Unfortunately, this P is typically overlooked and gets the least amount of attention than all of the other ST 6 P's. When preparing your business to sell, do not neglect your process, because it can have a huge impact on how profitable and efficient your business is, which will translate into how much you can realistically ask a buyer to purchase your business for when it comes time to putting your company on the market. Your process should be efficient and should start and end with the customer experience in mind. If you are able to get this part right, your business will grow exponentially, and you will earn top dollar at the closing table.

DID YOU KNOW?

- According to Process Street,
  - The predicted value of the business process market by 2023 is expected to reach $16 billion.
  - NASA's lack of processes caused a mistake resulting in the $193 million Mars Climate Orbiter satellite disintegrating.
  - Taco Bell went from losing money to being worth $1.98 billion in thirty years by reengineering their core processes.
  - Only 4 percent of companies measure and manage their documented processes.

IMPLEMENTATION IS KEY

To further explore the lessons learned in this chapter, implement the following:

- Review your processes, and make sure they are designed with the customer experience in mind.
- Ensure that your processes are efficient and productive. If necessary, make adjustments.
- Document your processes in a policy and procedure manual, and ensure your employees are trained on them.
- Incorporate two books in your company: One titled *The Book of WOW*, the other called *The Book of Un-WOW*. Use the first to encourage your team members to build morale, ownership, and teamwork by documenting outstanding processes that help enhance the client experience and ensure the company improves quality, efficiency, and productivity. The second book is designed for employees to document anything that did not work and caused customer dissatisfaction, inefficiency, and loss of productivity.

For free material on creating your own "books of WOW and Un-WOW,"
visit SeilerTuckerAcademy.com.

Proprietary

*"It takes 20 years to build a reputation and five minutes to ruin it.
If you think about that, you'll do things differently."*
—Warren Buffett

Proprietary, or branding, is the next P. Brand awareness and name recognition are huge, being one of the largest value drivers in selling companies. The larger the brand, the higher the sales price. That being said, some very large brands are either going out of business or are already out of business. We mentioned some of these in golden nugget 6: Blockbuster, Toys "R" Us, Kmart, etc. These are all well-known brands, but unfortunately, they stopped innovating to appeal to today's consumer. These brands all became obsolete due to Internet giants, such as Amazon and eBay, who make it easy for customers to shop from home.

Let's look at Coca-Cola. This brand is huge and one of the few brands consistently recognized worldwide. No matter what language someone speaks, they all know the name Coke. According to *The New York Times,* the Coke brand alone is worth $79 billion. That price does not include the inventory, FF&E (furniture, fixtures, and equipment), real estate, and cash flow. If you build your brand, you can work toward building your millions and billions, as long as your company stays current.

BRAND LOYALTY VERSUS LOCATION LOYALTY

To succeed in building your brand, you should ask yourself if you have brand loyalty or location loyalty. We once sold a specialized publishing firm, for example, that dealt in individualized candy bar wrappers. This was one part of this company's work. It could create candy bar wrappers for any occasion.

The owner of this business lived in New Orleans, whereas the buyer was from California but wanted to move the business to Florida. This was not a problem, because the company had a loyal following (brand loyalty) and was not dependent on any single location (location loyalty), because its services were accessible no matter where it was located. We were able to sell this business for millions and relocate it to Florida.

Ask yourself whether your business is based on brand loyalty or location loyalty. Every business is unique. Some are predicated on a good location; some aren't. It depends on the industry. Because of this, it is important to know where your business lies.

Most retail businesses are dependent on location. Moving the business could be detrimental. Customers don't like change. They come with a set of behaviors, habits, and routines that are sometimes impossible to break. If the business truly has brand loyalty, however, the clients will follow. But if the business only has location loyalty, they won't. It's that simple.

We have seen businesses relocate and not miss a beat. They keep on making money. We have also seen other businesses relocate and go out of business. You need to know your customers. It is important to know if you have brand loyalty or location loyalty before selling your business. If your business is based on location loyalty rather than brand loyalty, you may want to consider hiring a professional to assist you in building your brand before or during the selling process. In addition to knowing if your business has brand versus location loyalty, consider the following questions.

DO YOU HAVE A BRICK-AND-MORTAR LOCATION?

With a brick-and-mortar location, it's important to have visible signage and an appealing location for your customers. If your business is in a high-traffic area with good signage, it will have more visibility and attract more customers. Strip malls, with high-visibility anchors such as Target, Walmart, or Starbucks, will work in your favor. If you are preparing to move to a brick-and-mortar location, think of visibility when selecting your place of business. Will prospects constantly walk by your business on the way to a coffee shop or grocery store? Will you have a lot of walk-in customers drawn to you by your location? If so, you have chosen a good location that will attract a steady stream of business.

DOES YOUR BUSINESS DEPEND ON ITS LOCATION?

If your location is essential to the success of your business, you should have a long-term lease that is transferable, or you should be able to sublease. If your business is dependent on location loyalty and the buyer cannot transfer the lease or negotiate a new lease with the landlord, you will have nothing to sell.

Keep in mind that locations are vulnerable to storms, fire, and crazy land-lords. If your business is predicated on location, check with an attorney to make sure your lease is recorded, in accordance with your state's specific laws. We have witnessed horrible situations where the business owner's lease was not recorded, the landlord sold the building, and the new owner of the building evicted all the tenants. Our firm will not take an engagement if the business is predicated on the location and the lease is not transferable or if the landlord will not allow a sublease or negotiate a new lease. It's simply too risky otherwise, and we have seen too many scenarios where this ends badly for the seller.

As you're probably gathering, landlords can make or break a deal. It is almost impossible to sell a business, for example, if the business owner is on a month-to-month lease and the landlord will not negotiate a new lease. Keep in mind that if you put your business on the market and have a month-to-month lease, the buyer can and will go behind your back and negotiate with the landlord. There is nothing you can do about it. If your business is location dependent, sign a lease and protect yourself before putting your business on the market.

HOW LONG HAS YOUR BUSINESS BEEN AT THIS LOCATION?

The answer to this question will often determine if you can relocate your business or not. Ask yourself this: Can you relocate the business? If so, how far can it be moved? If your business can be relocated anywhere in the United States, you will have a much larger buying pool. Relocatable businesses sell like hotcakes!

DO YOU OPERATE YOUR BUSINESS OUT OF YOUR HOME?

Many home-based businesses do very well and generate great profits. These types of businesses are great to sell, because there is no lease involved and they can be relocated.

Buyers are intrigued and interested in being able to run and operate their business from home. They can have the best of both worlds; a home-based business allows them to spend more time with their families. Some businesses operate in an office space in a separate building on the owner's land, typically close to the owner's home. This could be a good option for the buyer if the seller is willing to sell the building and its land or to lease the building to the buyer. Either option can work for both parties. Sometimes, the owner is willing to sell the office building on the land along with their home. This is another good option for a buyer, especially out-of-state buyers.

DO YOU OWN THE REAL ESTATE?

Owning the real estate where your business is located is a huge benefit for business owners. It increases options for potential buyers and enlarges the buyer pool, because a buyer might be interested in both the business and the real estate. Owning the real estate provides versatility. You can sell the building, lease to purchase, or simply lease the space to the buyer who is purchasing your business.

You can also sell the building to someone other than the buyer of your business. If your building is located on prime real estate, such as a corner location, that opens more possibilities for larger-type retail tenants, such as a drugstore, fast-food chains, or drive-up dry cleaners. If you can relocate the business, you can capitalize on selling both the business and the real estate (if you own it). Real estate needs an appraisal, however. If you do not have a recent appraisal, obtain one as soon as possible.

YEARS IN BUSINESS

How long a business has been in business is also part of its intellectual property and will help drive value. The longer you've been in business, weathering the storms, doing well, and making a good profit, the more you can maximize the value of your company. Established businesses are more attractive to buyers, because, as a general rule, they're less risky. However, not all businesses are equal. Depending on the type of business and its style of ownership, different advantages and risks appeal to different types of buyers. For example, we had a buyer looking at a distribution company that had been in business for decades and making a great profit. The buyer loved the history of the business. However, he felt that the business was at risk of going out of business because their customers were as old as the business, and the company did not do any marketing or innovation to attract the newest generation of consumers. Once those exiting customers aged out, there was no prospect of new ones. Therefore, the buyer felt he could buy the current business but would have to spend a lot of money on innovation and marketing to add to the old client base. Because this was more than he wanted to take on, he decided not to buy this business.

TRADEMARKS AND PATENTS

Trademarks and patents are big value drivers, and businesses with trademarks and patents will demand a much higher price for the company. This is because they distinguish a business from its competitors.

We worked with a manufacturing plant that had eighteen patents and some additional ones pending. We ended up selling this company for 65 percent more than the appraised price because of their patents. We had hundreds of buyers within a few months of marketing this company for sale. We had several letters of intent (LOI) and were able to close within a few months of our seller's engagement. Our client was ecstatic, because we were able to sell 70 percent of his company for a much higher price than what the business appraised for. In addition to a higher selling price, our client retained 30 percent of the business, keeping his six-figure salary plus benefits.

The key ingredient here is to make sure you engage a qualified M&A advisor that has years of experience in valuating intellectual property and driving value as a result. If you work with an inexperienced advisor, you will leave lots of money on the table.

CONTRACTS

Contracts are another significant value driver. Buyers want to buy a sustainable business that has contracts in place, because this helps to guarantee future income. However, one of the issues associated with contracts is that most of them are not transferable. And nontransferable contracts can stop a sale dead in its tracks. Many owners think their contracts are transferable; however, upon review, they find out they are not. Therefore, it's imperative to review your client contracts and master service agreements before selling your business. If they are nontransferable, you must revise your agreements and have your clients sign new ones, or they will need to sign a consent form agreeing to allow the contract to transfer to the new owner. If the clients will not agree to sign a new agreement or a consent form, the sale will have to be classified as a stock sale.

We once sold a medical transportation company that had over fifty contracts with medical providers. The partners were adamant that their contracts were transferable. However, upon further review, we determined they were not. We told the partners that they needed to amend the agreements to accommodate for transferability. They said they would, and months went by.

After several months, we brought them an asset purchase offer to buy their company. The offer was accepted, and we began due diligence. We quickly discovered that they had not revised their agreements and that none of their contracts were transferable. We were closing in a few weeks, and there was no way they could get their clients to agree this late in the game. Therefore, we had no choice than to convert the sale from an asset to a stock sale. The sellers were fortunate, because most buyers will not agree to a stock sale for a multitude of reasons that we will explore further in golden nugget 16.

DATABASES

Databases are another huge value driver and are too often overlooked and undervalued. Databases are golden nuggets and can add significant value and synergies to business buyers. Facebook is a great example of this.

Facebook bought WhatsApp for $19 billion. At the time, WhatsApp was operating in the red (losing money). Why did Facebook pay so much for a company that was hemorrhaging money? It's simple: Facebook was willing to pay top dollar for a company that had intellectual property.

Sometimes, the intellectual property is worth more to a strategic buyer than the cash flow it produces. WhatsApp had something that Facebook was willing to pay billions for: their database. WhatsApp had more users than Facebook; in fact, they had over a billion users. Facebook knew that, through synergies, they could monetize those billion users and that doing so would catapult their own growth.

Your customer base is your database. Make sure you organize your clients in a client relationship management system (CRM). One of our clients owned a welding supply company for decades. The company was doing well and generating a profit. But evaluating his ST 6 P's revealed that the business was a throwback to the predigital age. There was not a single computer on the premises. Everything was done the old-fashioned way: on paper. Inventory was tracked on sheets and forms. The names and contact information for hundreds of customers were handwritten in not just one Rolodex but ten. Luckily, a fire never broke out.

The client needed a technological and operational overhaul to be able to run on all cylinders, especially proprietary, but he refused to invest money or time to digitize everything. Many buyers wanted to purchase his database, because he had hundreds of valuable clients. Unfortunately, he didn't have one to sell.

This was a serious roadblock: A buyer would have to invest time, money, energy, and effort into bringing everything into the twenty-first century. I advised the owner to reduce the price of the business to compensate a new owner for making the necessary changes. Once he did this, we were able to sell the business.

We discussed the different types of buyers in golden nugget 4. Competitors and strategic buyers are always looking for companies that are congruent and have intellectual property they can add to their current business landscape to grow their companies to new heights. When preparing to sell your business, you can implement the changes and address which one of the ST 6 P's you are missing in order to maximize value, or you can do nothing and be forced to accept a lower price. It's your choice.

MENTORING CORNER

The importance proprietary assets has to the overall value of your business cannot be stressed enough. More than 80 percent of the market value of S&P 500 companies resides in intangible assets, or intellectual property. Whether it be brand value, your databases, your intellectual property assets, your location, or your strength of relationships, their inherent value is intangible, meaning they are not included as assets on your balance sheet. As intangible assets, they justify the difference between the book value of your assets on your balance sheet and the much higher sales price you deserve for your business. You may have heard of the term *business goodwill*, which also refers to this difference.

Why is intellectual property so important to business valuation and your sales price? There are three primary reasons. Most significantly, obtaining exclusive rights to intellectual property is the primary mechanism for creating *sustainable competitive advantage*. Let's face it: If the product or service provided by a business can simply be replicated by competitors, the business is not worth as much as it would be if competitors are legally prevented from copying the product or service. Second, intellectual property can also be a demonstrative asset, easily presented to and recognized by potential purchasers. And third, intellectual property can also be the source of additional streams of income through a licensing or franchising program. Let's explore this concept further.

continued

COMPETITIVE ADVANTAGE

The success of a business can almost always be attributed to some form of advantage over its competition. This is known as a *competitive advantage*. There are two basic sources of competitive advantage: things that make your customers want to do business with you rather than the competition and things that give you better margins. The value of that competitive advantage to your business (and, ultimately, to the purchaser of your business) is, in large part, a function of whether that competitive advantage can be sustained over time. It is a function of the context of the sale of your business in the face of a change of ownership, personnel, or location.

Generally, sustainable competitive advantage involves one of two scenarios. The first is long-term contracts or government permits that create an exclusive right to something. Examples of exclusive rights that add value to your business are a necessary resource or distribution channel. The second scenario is that the business owns or has the rights to some form of *intellectual property*. This includes any intangible assets resulting from creativity, innovation, knowledge, and good relationships. Some examples are information and data, expertise and know-how, invention, designs, reputation and right of publicity, goodwill and associated trademarks, service marks and trade dress, works of authorship, and mask works. Domain names, telephone numbers, and addresses can also be intangible assets.

In order to sustain the competitive advantage, a foundation must be laid and steps must be taken to establish exclusive rights to the intellectual property. There are a number of different legal mechanisms for establishing exclusive rights in the different types of intellectual property. These include trade secret, utility patent, design patent, trademark copyright, and mask work protection.

Your business, particularly when you are thinking about or preparing to sell, should consciously and systematically identify all sources of competitive advantage and potential intellectual property assets, then take the necessary steps to establish, to the greatest extent possible, exclusive rights. Better yet, run your business with a conscious eye toward creating intellectual property. Regular consultation with a mentor or intellectual property professional can greatly facilitate this process.

The following chart, developed by the internationally recognized intellectual property attorney Michael A. Lechter, is a great reference tool; it

continued on page 93

INTELLECTUAL PROPERTY CHART

CATEGORY OF INTELLECTUAL PROPERTY	EXAMPLES	POTENTIALLY APPLICABLE PROTECTION
Nonproprietary information, data, and know-how (generally known or ascertainable from public sources)	General knowledge of industry, industry practices, and available resources (e.g., vendors, published specifications of parts or components) Expertise in conventional operation of equipment or standard industry processes	Goodwill (employee retention), institutionalization (possession by a number of people within business), memorialization (documentation and recording), reasonable agreement provisions (noncompetition, nonsolicitation, repayment of training expenses)
Proprietary information, data, and know-how (not generally known and not readily reverse engineerable or ascertainable from public sources)	Manufacturing processes employed by company; business systems and practices employed by company; unpublished business and technical documents, drawings, and blueprints; internal costs; marketing strategies and plans; business strategies and plans; financial information, budgets, costing and pricing methods; company vendor lists; unpublished parts lists for specific products and part tolerances; customer- and supplier-specific information and preferences; expertise regarding nonstandard use of equipment or particular uses of equipment by the company; algorithms, criteria, formulas, recipes (not readily reverse engineerable); unpublished research and development efforts, discoveries, results, and data and data collections	Goodwill (employee retention), reasonable agreement provisions (noncompetition, nonsolicitation, confidentiality, and limitations on use), trade secrets, copyrights (as to unpublished documents or works of authorship)

continued

CATEGORY OF INTELLECTUAL PROPERTY	EXAMPLES	POTENTIALLY APPLICABLE PROTECTION
Invention	Innovations, new developments, features, or functionality in products, manufacturing processes, and business processes involving technological elements	Trade secrets, utility patents
Industrial designs (nonfunctional appearance)	Design elements or appearance of products, packaging	Design patent, copyrights
Works of authorship (product of creative expression, such as literature, music, art, and graphic designs)	Business and technical documents, manuals (assembly, instruction, operation, etc.); brochures, marketing materials, and advertising copy; drawings and blueprints; memoranda and correspondence; photographs and images	Copyrights, trade secrets (unpublished works)
Mask works (representations of semiconductor chip topography)	Drawings showing semiconductor chip topography, databases used to produce semiconductor chips	Mask work protection, trade secrets (as to nonascertainable chips)
Goodwill, reputation, and trademarks	Words and logos associated with company or products by consumers; distinctive appearance of elements of product, packaging, or services (trade dress); historical good relationships; reputation for quality product or services	Reasonable agreements, trademarks

summarizes the different types of intellectual property, provides examples, and identifies the applicable protection mechanisms.

In preparing your business for sale, carefully reviewing and identifying your intellectual property can increase the valuation of your business dramatically. When doing so, ask yourself the following questions:

- Is there something that can be done to prevent your competitors from appropriating your intellectual property?

- Can you identify why customers come to your business rather than go to your competitors?

- What gives you your competitive advantage?

- Is there something about the way you do business, such as how you offer your products or services, that your consumers prefer over what your competitors do?

 KNOW MORE TO EXIT RICH

In this chapter, we learned about the fourth P, proprietary. As we discussed, brand awareness and name recognition are one of the largest value drivers when selling your business. So that you can command the highest sales price for your business, you will want to make sure that your brand and name recognition are strong. To do this, get to know your competition, stay relevant and current with economic and technological trends, take steps to market and promote your company, and make sure that you protect your brand with patents or trademarks to ensure that no one else walks away with your good idea and, eventually, your money.

DID YOU KNOW?

- According to Salesforce, 74 percent of people are likely to switch brands if they find the purchasing process too difficult.

- According to Help Scout, Americans are more likely to post about good experiences (53 percent) than poor experiences (35 percent) on social media.

- According to Label Insight, 94 percent of all consumers are more likely to be loyal to a brand that commits to full transparency.

- According to Brand Buddha, 33 percent of the top one hundred brands use the color blue in their logo.

- According to Crowdspring, although consumers form impressions of a brand's logo within ten seconds, it takes five to seven times for consumers to remember the logo.

- According to Sweor, it takes about fifty milliseconds for users to form an opinion about your website, determining whether they like your site or not and whether they'll stay or leave.

- According to Adobe, 38 percent of people will stop engaging with a website if the content or layout is unattractive.

IMPLEMENTATION IS KEY

To further explore the lessons learned in this chapter, implement the following: Review your intellectual property before putting your business up for sale, and ask yourself these questions:

- Do you have trademarks or trade secrets?
- Is your business based on brand loyalty or location loyalty?
- Do you have any patents or patents pending?
- Does your company have name recognition?
- Does your business have brand awareness?

- How long have you been in business?
- Do you have contracts, and are they transferable?
- Do you have a database? If so, how many contacts do you have, and have they been continually updated?

To rank the proprietary power of your brand, go to SeilerTuckerAcademy.com and download your free checklist to see how you rank!

9

 **Patrons**

*"We see our customers as invited guests to a party,
and we are the hosts. It's our job every day to make every
important aspect of the customer experience a little bit better."*

—Jeff Bezos

The most important thing in business is customers, which is our next P—patrons. Without customers to fuel your business, you will run out of gas, because you will not have any business. Most businesses have customers. However, those customers can make a business either more or less valuable, depending on how well you cater to them. Therefore, it is important to know your customer base, because it can dictate your company's overall value.

Customers fall into three different categories:

- Loyalty
- Convenience
- Price consciousness

LOYALTY

Loyal clients will stay with a business and continue to purchase their goods and services, regardless of quality. Take a look at your current business model. Are you working to establish brand loyalty, or is your focus elsewhere? Review your current client base. Are you constantly replacing clients with new customers because your client retention is lacking? If you have great client retention, then ask yourself why. Is it because you have the best customer service, the best product, and the best price? It's important to know why you do and do not have customer loyalty.

Apple is notorious for doing everything to push a customer into the arms of another brand. They purposely add updates that slow your phone down so you'll go out and buy another one. Their batteries start dying earlier and earlier. Consumers constantly complain about Apple phones; however, you don't see them running out to buy another brand. Why is that? It's because customers are addicted to the Apple brand. They could go out and buy a better phone with a faster speed and a longer shelf life, but they don't, because they are diehard Apple fans.

Apple has done a great job of creating brand advocacy, which is the best brand loyalty you can possibly build. As a result, Apple clients will go way out of their way to purchase a new iPhone or iPad. And they will wait in long lines for hours just to be the first to purchase the latest and greatest Apple product.

CONVENIENCE

These customers have no loyalty and will only buy from companies that provide great convenience. They want something that is easy and don't want to go out of their way to purchase products and services. When looking over your business model, determine whether convenience is important to your business or whether it makes more sense to focus on the other categories.

A customer uses a dry cleaner that picks up and delivers. This dry cleaner is much more expensive than their local drive-through; however, they don't want to load and unload their clothes from their house to their car. They are willing to pay more for convenience. These consumers are not loyal and will switch dry cleaners in an instant if a less expensive cleaner provides the same level of convenience.

PRICE CONSCIOUSNESS

These buyers buy based only on price. They will travel all over town, going from business to business to get the best price. Is price a driving factor in your business? If so, you will need to stay current on price to remain competitive in the marketplace. However, you should also ask yourself whether focusing on this category will provide you with the most value for your business in the long term.

Michelle has a friend who will burn up a tank of gas driving all over town, going into several grocery stores to save a few pennies. Her friend does not care that it costs her more in gas money to save a little. In her mind, it's the principle of saving money that causes her to be so unreasonable.

By now, we're sure you have determined which customer drives the most value in a business buyer's mind. It's obviously the Apple or brand-loyal client that will drive the higher price when selling your company. Whenever possible and for maximum value, focus on brand loyalty rather than price and convenience when preparing your business for sale.

CUSTOMER CONCENTRATION

In addition to valuating the types of customers a business has, the business buyer also wants to look at which customers make up what percentage of the revenues. It's typically the 80/20 rule, where 80 percent of your revenue comes from 20 percent of your clients—otherwise known as customer concentration. This historic formula is what scares business buyers, because if 80 percent of your business comes from 20 percent of your customers, what happens if you lose 5 to 10 percent of your customer base and they have not been replaced? Customer concentration is the number-one issue that will cause a buyer to run away from the sale of your business.

We worked with a specialty boutique advertising agency that wanted to sell their business. This business operated on some of the ST 6 P's. They had talented tenured employees, their service was in demand, their processes were efficient, and they were profitable. What they did not have were patrons. They only had five clients, and they were not diversified. They specialized in providing marketing services for casinos, which is a great business, but all their customers were in only one industry. During the time we worked together, they lost two big clients, which left them with only three casinos to service. Their revenue dramatically decreased, but the expenses, unfortunately, stayed the same.

Needless to say, as their profits went down and overhead stayed the same, no one wanted to buy their company. This business was unlikely to sell when they only had five casinos, but after losing two, it was not sellable at all. The only thing we could do was merge them with another advertising agency.

The other agency had a different problem. They had diversified clients but not enough talented employees to service those clients. Their weakness— a lack of employees, people, the first P—was our client's strength, and our client's lack of customers—the fifth P, patrons—was their strength. It was a business match made in heaven. Obviously, there were other obstacles we had to overcome, but they were a good strategic fit. However, it is rare to find a business match so quickly. It did work out in this instance, but that's not always the case. Therefore, it's imperative to make sure that your customer base is diversified and that you don't have customer concentration.

Customer concentration only attracts a competitor or strategic buyer that is buying a specific client base. For instance, we sold a $15 million oil manufacturing plant that had all their revenue tied up in one client, BP. Approximately 60 percent of their revenues were tied up in BP's master service agreement. Most buyers would not touch this company with a ten-foot pole, because they would be fearful of losing BP, thus losing 60-plus percent of the revenue. We had over seven hundred buyers look at the business, and most of them were concerned about the customer concentration.

As a result of our hard work and marketing efforts, we were able to find a strategic buyer that was in the same industry with a similar product. They had been trying to win over the BP contract for years and could never seem to get their foot in the door. Like Facebook, they knew that if they could buy the company and nurture the business's current relationship with BP, they could finally get their services in the door. They could then monetize that relationship, which would improve the ROI on the purchase of the new business.

Strategic buyers always look for synergies in employees, clients, databases, and congruent revenues. Most want to take advantage of economies of scale. The issue with this particular company is that they had a master service agreement with BP that was not transferable. The sellers did everything in their power to get BP to revise the agreement and make it transferable. One partner went so far as to buy wine and chocolates for the female decision maker and, according to him, get down on one knee and propose. Unfortunately, nothing was working. When it came time to close on the sale, they still had not gotten BP to agree to the transfer. The buyers were desperate to close, so we initiated a transition service agreement. This allowed the buyers to buy the business and continue to service them under the old master service agreement. This is a risky move, but the buyers were willing to take the risk. Fortunately, it paid off in a big way.

Most buyers will not buy a business with customer concentration. If they do, they will require their attorney to craft language into the closing documents, such as reps and warranties or a discount in future payments, to protect them from overpaying if clients walk after the sale.

Recently, we sold an office supply company that had been in business since the 1950s. Talk about customer concentration; as much as 60 percent of its business was tied up in government contracts. Such government contracts are negotiated by a third-party company and typically renewed every two to three years. The problem here was that 12 percent of this company's business came from a seller's negotiated contract. This contract was ending in a few months, and another contract that represented 5 percent of the seller's business was ending in a few days. The buyer negotiated an offer that would provide a price reduction if the seller couldn't renew these two contracts. The adjustments would decrease the amount of seller financing payments due to the seller on a monthly basis. Fortunately, the seller was able to renew both agreements and keep the original price.

Many buyers would want to decrease the sales price to accommodate the possibility of losing money. However, this is a much better negotiation tactic, because it allows the buyer to mitigate risk while the price remains the same (protecting the seller). It also offers the buyer protection in case the company loses customers or revenue.

Buyers are looking for the seller to give concessions if there is a chance that the revenue could decline based on the business's customer base. As we mentioned earlier, typically 80 percent of revenue comes from 20 percent of clients. Ask yourself this: Is a sizable percentage of your business tied up in one or two customers? If so, this could be a huge issue in your business and will send a red flag to prospective buyers. This is not good for business, because if you lose that one customer, you could be out of business.

Buyers will explore your client mix in the due diligence phase. They will look for a diversified customer mix. They don't want the seller's products and services to be tied to one or just a few customers. Buyers know if that client leaves, the business will take a huge hit and likely go out of business.

For example, if you are selling a hotel, a B&B, a daycare center, or an education business, most buyers will want to know what your occupancy or capacity rate is, or how many people you service. If your occupancy rate is high, you will obtain a higher selling price. If your occupancy rate is low, however, you'll need to figure out the problem and stop the bleeding. Otherwise, you are going to have to sell for less.

QUESTIONS TO DETERMINE YOUR CUSTOMER CONCENTRATION

Replacing customers is one of the most expensive line items in running a business, so it is important to determine your customer concentration. To do this, ask yourself these questions:

- How many clients do you lose a year?
- How much money does it cost you to replace a client?
- Do you lose customers due to the economy?
- Do you lose customers due to poor service and lack of quality control?
- Do you lose customers due to employee turnover?

- What is your retention rate?

- Do your clients speak highly of you and refer your products and services to their friends, family, and colleagues?

- What percentage of your business comes from referrals?

- What is your occupancy rate?

- Who is your client base?

- Do you have a diversified client base?

- Do you have residential or commercial clients?

- Do you have wholesale or retail clients?

- What is your company's relationship with your clients? Do you have a one-on-one relationship with your customers, or do you barely see them?

- Are your clients loyal to you, your products, and your services?

- What is the demographic makeup of your clients?

- Are most of your customers older? If so, you might want to explore some options to market your products and services to younger generations.

- Is your customer base mostly made up of younger individuals who do not have a great deal of disposable income? If so, you might want to market your products and services to people who may have more disposable income. To be diversified, it is prudent to market your products and services to a wide range of generations.

- Are you marketing and innovating your products or services to appeal to newer generations?

- Are most of your clients female or male? Are your products and services gender specific, or are your products and services versatile enough to appeal to the masses?

- Who can afford to purchase your products and services? For example, do your products and services appeal to blue-collar individuals or individuals with a higher disposable income?

- What is the geographical area in which consumers travel to buy products or services from your business?

- What is the radius that your products and services draw from? Can you expand your marketing to attract buyers from a larger radius, or can you invest more advertising dollars into local or niche market areas to increase visibility and gain more market share?

- Will an increase in gas prices cause your clients to avoid traveling to your business to purchase your products and services? If so, can you sell to your customers via the Internet and ship products directly to them?

- What percentage of your business is repeat business?

- What is the tenure of your clients?

- Do you have customer contracts in place, and are they transferable?

MENTORING CORNER

The demographics of your customer base are important for you to know, as well as to monitor. In addition, having a documented system of your customer journey from lead generation, customer acquisition, and sales to repeat sales and ongoing customer service will be important to a potential buyer. This is especially true if your business provides consumable products where your customers are repeat buyers and, even better, where they are on automatic shipping programs. This greatly elevates the lifetime value of your customers.

LOCATION AND CUSTOMER CONCENTRATION

As you go through the process of documenting your customer demographics and customer journey, you will identify potential problems as well as opportunities, and often both, depending on the potential buyer. Say, for instance, your business operates primarily in the southwestern United States. A buyer in Georgia may lose interest because of the logistics of

continued

acquiring you. However, perhaps a buyer in New York has been looking for expansion in the Southwest, and you are a perfect acquisition for them.

Location, whether domestic or international, is always an important consideration as to market penetration. But industry penetration can also be important. If your business is primarily in the auto industry, for example, and the buyer wants to break into that industry with their own products, they will see your customer base as a huge opportunity.

While a high concentration of your sales coming from only a few customers is problematic in almost all cases, if those customers have contractually committed to ongoing purchases for a period of time, that concern can be mitigated. Or if those few customers fill a gap or create a new market for the potential buyer, it may not be seen as a problem but as an opportunity.

MONITOR YOUR ONLINE PRESENCE

Your customer service systems can be great assets or problematic. With so many online reviews available today, you should have a system in place that monitors your online presence, which includes any online reviews. Any complaints should be quickly addressed, and compliments should be applauded. Customers who become raving fans become your best market- ing tools, so do everything you can to build a strong presence and cus- tomer base online.

 KNOW MORE TO EXIT RICH

In this chapter, we covered the fifth P, patrons. You learned the importance of having brand-loyal customers to fuel your business. By getting to know your customer base, you can take the necessary steps to increase your brand loyalty, and, in turn, your company's overall value, which will translate into extra dol- lars when you sell.

DID YOU KNOW?

- According to American Express, seven out of ten US consumers say they've spent more money to do business with a company that delivers great service.

- According to *Harvard Business Review*, it is anywhere from five to twenty-five times more expensive to acquire a new customer than it is to keep a current one.

- According to *Reader's Digest*, Starbucks' round tables were created specifically so customers would feel less alone.

- According to Help Scout, US companies lose more than $62 billion annually due to poor customer service.

- According to *Harvard Business Review*, increasing customer retention rates by 5 percent increases profits anywhere from 25 to 95 percent.

- According to Help Scout, after one negative experience, 51 percent of customers will never do business with that company again.

- According to Help Scout, companies that make a concerted effort to improve their customer experience also see employee engagement rates go up by an average of 20 percent.

IMPLEMENTATION IS KEY

To further explore the lessons learned in this chapter, implement the following:

- Review your client base.
- Know your customer concentration.
- If you have customer concentration, start diversifying immediately.
- Know your ideal client.
- Know your customer acquisition cost.
- Innovate to stay relevant and appeal to consumers.
- Market to your targeted client base.

- Implement a client loyalty program.

- Improve customer service.

- Implement a customer service policy, setting forth how you address customer dissatisfaction in your business.

To watch a free training video by Michelle on knowing how to create client diversification and ensure client loyalty, visit SeilerTuckerAcademy.com.

⑩

 **Profits**

"Rule No. 1: Never lose money.
Rule No. 2: Never forget rule No. 1."
—Warren Buffett

We are now going to discuss the final P in the 6 P Method. All of the P's are crucial to the success of a business. Profits, however, are the most profound P, because without them, your business will not be sustainable, and you will not be able to sell it for a profit, unless you have lots of intellectual property, as in the case of WhatsApp.

If you asked people on the street, "Do you think businesses make money?" most will tell you yes, business owners are rich; they make lots of money. It's a huge misconception that all businesses are profitable; many are not. We have actually seen businesses gross millions only to make little to no profit.

Let's look at some examples of businesses you would naturally think are rolling in the dough.

FACEBOOK

In its beginning stages, Facebook was not making any money; in fact, they were bleeding. Their entire business model was based on making connections, not making money; they had not created a mechanism to monetize their service. Their lack of ability to make money was hugely criticized by investors on Wall Street for years. The first year Facebook tried to generate revenue through advertisements was 2012. Some of their angel investors, Peter Thiel (2004), Greylock Partners (2006), Accel Partners (2005), and Meritech Capital (2006), wanted them to start generating revenue through advertisements sooner.

They knew the importance of profits and were able to finally turn their ability to connect people into their ability to make billions by enticing advertisers to advertise to their target audience. Today, Facebook is one of the best advertising platforms in the world.

WHATSAPP

Before its sale to Facebook, WhatsApp was hemorrhaging money, with no end in sight. WhatsApp reported just over $10 million in revenue in 2013 and a total net loss of $138 million for the year. A big part of that loss, about $98.8 million, came in the form of stock-based compensation. Even then, the company was operating at about a $40 million loss. Fortunately for the company, Facebook saw a gold mine sitting in their database and purchased them outright in 2014.

NEIMAN MARCUS

Credit Risk Monitor warned in January that Neiman Marcus's risk of declaring bankruptcy in 2019 was as high as 50 percent. Yes, the company's sales for the quarter ending in October of 2018 were up for the first time in a long time. But earnings were still lower on a year-over-year basis. The retail math, unfortunately, just doesn't work unless a company can sell more merchandise to more customers at higher prices. As a result, the company had to pull out all the stops and spend heavily to increase revenue growth, which enabled them to stay in business.

GYMBOREE GROUP

The children's clothing retailer is facing its second round of bankruptcy in two years, after failed attempts to globalize and rebrand. The company's combination of failure to compete with other brands in its division and poor sales have left them with no choice but to make extensive discounts on merchandise and to close over three hundred stores since 2017. After declaring bankruptcy in 2017, the company received an $85 million new-term loan from Goldman Sachs and access to a $200 million revolving credit facility from Bank of America Merrill Lynch and Citizens. The group's current liabilities are $10,000,001 to $50 million, but no new levels of success have been made after the initial bankruptcy.

QUIZNOS

The sandwich chain has fallen from once operating five thousand stores at their peak to around 2,100, with hundreds of other locations close to shutting down. The Denver-based chain recently missed payment on a loan and is working to restructure its nearly $600 million in debt. This type of restructuring can happen when your sixth P is weak.

SNAPCHAT

After falling more than 5 percent, Snap Inc. shares hit $7.08 during midday trading in October 2018. Snap shares are down 52 percent since the start of 2018. Snap started 2019 with $2 billion in cash and burned about $500 million by November 2019—giving it another year or two of runway at its current pace. Analysts estimate a $1.5 billion loss in 2019 for Snap due to the company's inability to generate a strong sixth P.

GUESS

This once-iconic apparel brand is suffering due to the retail apocalypse led by online shopping and Amazon.com. As a result, revenue has been falling at an average annual pace of 3.8 percent a year for the last half decade. Due to a decline in their sixth P, the company's earnings per share has declined by ten times that annual rate—nearly 40 percent yearly—over that same period.

NORDSTROM

The once-impressive retail business is currently in a decline. The company's stock, which hit all-time highs as recently as 2015, is under pressure from decelerating sales growth and falling margins, with a debt-equity ratio of 3.2, especially in a rising-rate environment. Yet another example of what can happen when your business is suffering from a week sixth P.

COMPANY CYCLES

Businesses go through cycles, and many companies will not generate profits in the first few years, which is why they must have enough working capital to weather the financial storm. It's quite comical, because many experts will say a company went out of business because it did not have a good business plan. Having a good business plan has little to nothing to do with the success of a business. We do believe that businesses should have a good business plan; however, the lack of one is not the reason companies go out of business. Businesses go out of business because they run out of money, which comes in from investors or company profits.

As in one's life, businesses go through cycles—from being born to, unfortunately, dying. These cycles are as follows:

- Newborn
- Infant
- Toddler
- Teenager
- Young adult
- Adult
- Senior citizen
- Death

NEWBORN

This is the incubator stage, where an idea is born and a business is started. Most business babies never make it out of the incubator stage, because the creator is usually looking for venture capital and can never seem to raise enough to nourish and grow their baby.

INFANT

This is the stage that the business baby has stumbled out of the incubator but needs money and expertise to grow.

TODDLER

This stage is where the business baby is taking its first steps, learning to talk, and starting to show some real growth. However, this is still a critical time, because the business toddler is not stable and the profits, if any, are not sustainable.

TEENAGER

This stage is where the business baby is growing and making its footprint in the business world; however, it is still fragile because with one misstep it can be out of business. This stage could generate profits; however, the teenager is at risk for making poor financial decisions.

YOUNG ADULT

In this stage, the business baby is making real progress and has its foothold in the business world. However, it is still learning and tends to be reckless in decision making.

ADULT

By this stage, the business baby has figured out how to run a business. It is operating on all the ST 6 P's and generating profits.

SENIOR CITIZEN

In this stage, the business is either growing or dying. If it is dying, it means the business babies have lost their footing or lost faith in their consumers' minds, brand awareness, or name recognition; but most importantly, they are losing profits. If the business is growing, it is because it is continuing to grow or scale from all the ST 6 P's, operating efficiently with seasoned professional management.

Businesses will cycle back and forth through these stages for a multitude of reasons. A business could revert to the toddler stage, for example, due to changes in the economy, government, regulations, employees, natural disasters, and personal issues.

DEATH

Senior citizen businesses that have been around for decades will typically revert back to infancy, end up on life support, and eventually die. Again, the reason these businesses fail is that they neglect to innovate and market in order to stay relevant to new generations and new consumers. They may fail to stay relevant, but their competition didn't, and that competition ended up with their market share as a result. We always tell our clients, "Stop letting the competitors eat off your plate!"

Some examples of senior citizen businesses that were once in their prime but that are now dead to most consumers include these:

- Toys "R" Us

- Montgomery Ward

- Kmart

- Blockbuster

Michelle recently met a lady at a conference where she was speaking. She called and asked Michelle to help rescue her father and his business. He was about to file for bankruptcy and lose everything. Her father was a pharmacist who had started a pharmacy over sixty years ago in a small town in New Jersey. His pharmacy had been swallowed up by Walgreens on one corner and CVS on the next. In addition to those two, Walmart was down the street. Needless to say, he did nothing to innovate and market to stay relevant in the minds of consumers. Unfortunately, it was too late to save his business; he had been losing profits for years. During that time, he had spent all the family's savings and mortgaged the family home. His business was on life support until it eventually died. The big problem is that most businesses don't simply die and get buried. They also often take the family's assets along with it.

KNOW YOUR NUMBERS

Again, in the 6 P Method, profits are huge, and this P is a measuring stick to see how well the business is and what stage it is in. You would think that business owners would always be focused on the bottom line; however, most of them are not. Many don't even notice there is an issue until it's too late. Business owners are so used to robbing Peter to pay Paul that they don't see the warning signs, such as unpaid invoices, checks not adding up, and mistakes on the general ledger, until it's too late. Countless cases are reported each year of employee embezzlement. Millions of dollars are stolen from companies, and the employer never knew. In some cases, the theft went on for years before the employer or their professional team caught the crooked employee. This happens when the owners are so busy running their business that they are not paying attention to the numbers, which are the first warning signs of theft.

Profits are the measuring stick, the thermometer to gauge how well the business is doing. It's unfortunate that many business owners are completely clueless about their numbers. To generate profits, you should always know the following numbers in your company:

- Gross revenues
- The cost of goods
- The gross profit margin
- Your industry's average profit margin
- Business expenses
- Personal expenses
- Nonrecurring expenses
- Cash flow

- Net income
- EBITDA

NET INCOME

Net income can be deceiving. The net income of a company is its profit. The terminology is influenced by its source, which is the company's income statement. This statement shows income at the top—namely, the company's revenues. Items are then deducted from this income—costs for raw materials, wages, supplies, purchased services, rents, lease payments, executive salaries, marketing expenses, management overhead, and depreciation. At each point, the subtotals become less and less. At the very end, taxes are deducted. The last line of the income statement finally shows what is left over: net income. This is the company's profit, also known as *after-tax income*. Wall Street calls this number *earnings after tax* or *earnings* for short.

CASH FLOW STATEMENT

In financial accounting, a cash flow statement, also known as a statement of cash flows, is a financial statement that shows how changes in balance sheet accounts and income affect cash and cash equivalents. The cash flow statement breaks the analysis down to operating, investing, and financing activities. Cash flow is calculated by making certain adjustments to net income by adding or subtracting differences in revenue, expenses, and credit transactions (appearing on the balance sheet and income statement) resulting from transactions that occur from one period to the next.

KEY PERFORMANCE INDICATORS

You should also know your daily KPIs. Again, the numbers don't lie. You should review your dashboard daily to gauge how your business is performing. KPIs can indicate if your business is running on all six cylinders (ST 6 P's) or if the business needs a checkup. These should be able to gauge if the business is healthy, indicate warning signs, and let you know when your business is in the danger zone and needs an immediate tune-up or overhaul.

Many business owners get frustrated, upset, and angry when a business starts to drive into the danger zone. We always tell our clients not to get mad but, instead, to get the stats and hire a professional to get your business out of the danger zone. Many times, you need an outsider's perspective to identify the problems and implement solutions. A true expert will not treat the symptom but, rather, will fix the problem.

Now, profits are not always the reason businesses fail. But without profits, it's hard to fix the problem, as in the case of the pharmacy owner mentioned earlier. However, even if there are profits (money to fix the problem), most business owners don't have the expertise to identify the real problems. Most problems are hidden in the symptoms of what we perceive the actual problem to be when it's not the problem at all.

CASE STUDY: PLASTICS MANUFACTURING COMPANY

We had a plastics manufacturing company call us about selling their business. We asked the owner, "Why do you want to sell?" She stated, "Our company is not as profitable as it used to be, and we don't have the business acumen to fix and grow the company." Unfortunately, that was the symptom, not the problem. Let's apply her situation to the ST 6 P's and identify the real problems.

PEOPLE

They had over a hundred employees, many of which had been with the owners for decades, generating way above average pay for those positions. The owners (mostly due to their culture) felt obligated to keep raising their employees' salaries and benefits. Rewarding employee loyalty is a great concept. It's important to take care of your number-one P, people. However, you must also continue to grow the profits to be able to continue those high wages and stay profitable.

These overpaid positions could be replaced by machines and less expensive workers to improve efficiency and substantially decrease overhead. These overpaid employees were sucking the company dry, because the employees and owners were doing nothing to increase revenues, decrease overhead, and grow profits. As a result, this company became upside down in employee cost.

Having people is crucial in the 6 P Method; however, having the right people with the right compensation is even more critical. Business owners must watch their bottom line, and this means overseeing and overhauling compensation plans to maintain profitability. Without profits, you won't be able to keep your employees for long. Many business owners make the mistake of overcompensating employees to keep them happy. However, it's imperative that you reward loyal employees based on results, not just tenure and the fear that you're going to lose them.

PRODUCT

Their product was in demand but was at risk of being replaced with new packaging that is environmentally friendly.

PROCESS

The company lacked process, because manufacturing equipment could reduce overhead, reduce waste, and improve efficiencies and productivity. Their competitors offered better pricing, because they had less employee overhead.

PROPRIETARY

They had been in business for decades and had good brand recognition and name awareness.

PATRONS

They had no loyal clients. Most of their patrons were price conscious and shopped for the best deal.

PROFITS

They operated on a tight profit margin, leaving no room for waste and inefficiency.

THE OWNER'S PERCEIVED PROBLEM: DECREASED PROFITS

The owner called us to sell their company, because the company was losing money, and they were robbing their savings account to pay overhead. She stated a lack of profits as the problem. As you can clearly see, decreased profits were the symptom, not the problem. The actual problem was that they lacked most of the ST 6 P's, and their business was in the senior citizen stage.

THE ACTUAL PROBLEMS

Remember the issues that can cause a healthy adult company to become a senior citizen and eventually die? We noticed they were overpaying their employees, causing profits to rapidly decrease. In addition, their process was inefficient due to a lack of manufacturing equipment, and it continued to operate in dog years, not staying current. They also had no loyal patrons; their customers cared about cost over quality. And their profit margins were squeaky tight, allowing zero room for waste and inefficiency. Their profits continued to decrease as their employee cost skyrocketed over the average industry pay. Most importantly, their profit margin would not support over-paid employees. Their product was also at risk of being replaced with new environmentally conscious packaging.

This company had several problems. It was not only dying; it was taking the family assets to the grave with it. The owners were so buried in the stress of digging the company out of the financial hole that they could not see the problems and implement solutions to fix them. Instead, they were busy trying to keep their financial boat afloat, which is why they couldn't see the forest for the trees. That's why we always say, "When you're in the middle of fog, it's foggy!" In their case, profits were not the real problem—the lack of functioning on the ST 6 P's was.

However, as this example illustrates, a lack of profits is typically not the real problem. A lack of profits is always the symptom of not operating on all of the ST 6 P's. For instance, if your processes are not efficient, it will cost you money. If you did not properly trademark your company name or patent your product, this will cost you a lot of money in court to protect your intellectual property. And if you are lacking people in your company, then you are busy working in your business, not on it, which means you are not keeping your eyes on the profits.

THE BIG QUESTIONS ALL BUYERS ASK

As you can see from the above example, a lack of profits is the symptom of a poorly run company. However, if the company is still profitable and not operating on all the ST 6 P's, they won't be profitable for long, because profits in a poorly run company are not sustainable.

First and foremost, buyers are going to want to know if your business is profitable. That means more than just if you're in the red or black. Buyers want to clearly see and understand the systems and processes that are in place to generate that profit, so your financials really must be an open book.

When selling your business, buyers will ask a series of big questions, as outlined in the following list. Most business owners will need to review this list in great detail and clean their financial house or hire an expert to do so before placing the business on the market.

- Do you have clean financials?
- Do you show a profit?
- What is your gross income and expenses?
- What is your profit margin?
- What is your industry's average profit margin?
- How many revenue streams do you have?
- Do you take a salary?
- Are your employee compensations in line with the rest of your industry?
- Are you up-to-date on your taxes, both income taxes and employment taxes?
- Are you reporting everything?
- Do you operate on a calendar year or a fiscal year?
- Is your business predicated on inventory?
- What are your assets?

- What are your inventory holdings?

- What is the value of your furniture, fixtures, and equipment (FF&E)?

- Do you have accounts receivable?

- What are your average accounts receivable?

- Is your average collection rate above 90 percent?

- Do you have customer contracts in place?

- What is your debt?

- Are you on a cash or accrual accounting basis?

MENTORING CORNER

Your financials are the thermometer for your business. Therefore, it is imperative to have qualified employees preparing your financials and experienced advisors helping you interpret them to identify trends that are both negative and positive. While your balance sheet is a snapshot of your business finances (assets, liabilities, and net worth) on a given day, your income statement shows the financial results for your operations over a period of time.

CASH FLOW
If your business sales tend to fluctuate (e.g., a retail store with concentrated sales in the fourth quarter), it is important to plan your cash flow needs accordingly. Many businesses struggle because they do not properly manage cash flow. For instance, you may have a successful campaign in marketing that generates a spike in sales, but you do not have sufficient cash on hand to produce the inventory needed to fill the orders. This is a problem. This is why having established KPIs with a regular reporting process like a dashboard will help you spot issues quickly so corrections can be made before the issues become problematic.

CONSIDER AUDITED FINANCIALS
A potential buyer will want dependable and verifiable financial statements, as well as tax returns, to review. If you have the ability to provide audited financials, it will definitely help the due diligence process.

continued

> **BE PREPARED**
>
> In addition to providing audited financials, you'll want to be prepared to share your compensation as an owner, as well as any of your personal expenses paid by the company, because a buyer will want to make sure these amounts are both reasonable and consistent for your industry.
>
> You'll also want to review your contracts, long-term liabilities, and banking relationships to make sure you know how they would be affected by a potential sale of your business. For instance, you may find that a long-term liability of the business requires payment in full in the event of a change of ownership. A proper review of these documents now can help prevent unwanted surprises later.

 KNOW MORE TO EXIT RICH

You have now learned about how each of the ST 6 P's works to help you prepare your business for a profitable sale. In this chapter, we covered the last P, profits. While all of the P's are important to the overall success of your business, profits are the most impactful. Without them, your business will not be sustainable, and you will not be able to sell it for a profit. Stay on top of your financials, and know where your business is in its life cycle in case you need to make any adjustments to any of the other P's. Doing so will help you make your business as profitable and attractive as it can be to prospective buyers, translating into a greater return for you and, in turn, helping you to exit rich.

DID YOU KNOW?

- According to *Small Business Trends*, only 40 percent of small businesses are profitable.

- According to *Business Insider*, Walmart averages a profit of $1.8 million every hour.

- According to Think Gaming, Candy Crush brings in a reported $1.5 million a day in revenue.

IMPLEMENTATION IS KEY

To further explore the lessons learned in this chapter, implement the following:

- Always know your numbers.
- Every month make sure your invoices are getting paid, your accounts balance, and your general ledger is accurate.
- Employ a third-party system of checks and balances and have a book-keeper or CPA check your books regularly.
- Start using a cash flow statement in your business.
- Know your industry profit margins and measure them against yours.
- Compare your overhead to that of your competitors.
- Review your KPIs daily.
- Clean your financial house.

For free access to an exclusive training video by Michelle about how profits are never the problem, but always a symptom of not operating on all ST 6 P's, please go to SeilerTuckerAcademy.com.

You can also visit SeilerTuckerAcademy.com for free access to "The 10 Biggest Profit Mistakes."

PART 3

SELLING YOUR BUSINESS

11

Normalizing Your Financials

"Nobody ever lost money taking a profit."
—Bernard Baruch

Thus far, we have talked about different types of businesses and the different types of buyers. We have discussed the ST 6 P's, along with a multitude of golden nuggets that will help your business sell for more than others. The last P, profits, is usually disguised as expenses on the tax returns, which dramatically decreases a company's profits on paper.

Individuals told Michelle that the title of her first book, *Sell Your Business for More than It's Worth,* was deceiving. They said, "You need to be fair to the buyer and sell a business for what it's worth, not for more." Her response has always been, "A business is worth very little on paper, as many owners don't show much of a profit, but by the time we are done normalizing the financials, the business is making significant profits. This is how we are able to sell a business for more than it's worth on paper."

Ultimately, a business is worth what a buyer is willing to pay for it. And we can't evaluate what the business is worth without normalizing the financials of our client's business. We go through the tedious process of normalizing the financials with each of our clients. In this process, we go through each line item on the seller's profit and loss statements (P&L) and tax returns and add back the owner's personal and nonrecurring expenses. It's this process that determines the seller's true adjusted EBITDA.

Many businesses are worth nothing on paper. However, add-backs adjust profits upward. You must know your add-backs and report all of your income, or you will lose huge profits on the sale of your business. Therefore, it's imperative that you engage an M&A advisor or business broker to normalize the financials.

There are over thirty million businesses in the United States, and 99.9 percent are small businesses (firms with fewer than five hundred employees), according to the Office of Advocacy estimates. Small business owners cannot afford to stay in business if they don't realize a profit to take care of their family and their living expenses.

One of the biggest problems with keeping sloppy books and records is tracking the owner's expenses and other extraneous and one-time expenses. Business owners typically have amnesia when it comes to remembering what they are running through their company. We work with our clients to identify all nonbusiness expenses. We do not add back personal and nonrecurring expenses if the seller can't prove the add-backs to us. Therefore, buyers and their teams will need to go through all of the expenses during due diligence to prove the legitimacy of each add-back.

This can get painful when the seller reveals, line item by line item, what they've bought and how much they've funneled through the company. If your business doesn't show a healthy profit on its tax returns, it's almost impossible to sell the business without going through this exercise—all because you've been running personal expenses through the company and using cash to pay bills.

These personal expenses can include the following:

- Auto expenses

- Travel

- Car insurance

- Gas for all family members' cars

- Health insurance

- Retirement funds

- Home remodeling

- Meals

- Entertainment or memberships

- Phones

- Donations

- Tuition

- Kids' uniforms

We've seen it all. There are many more personal expenses that business owners run through their companies. The business owner may be able to justify these expenses as business expenses, but to a potential buyer, they will be seen as unnecessary expenses that burden the underlying profit of the business, therefore creating the need for adjustment in EBITDA and in the purchase price.

Nonrecurring expenses are typically a one-time expense. For example, Michelle moved her office after being in the same location for seventeen years. She spent over $60,000 in renovation and moving expenses. If Michelle were to sell her company, she would add back $60,000, as this was a one-time expense.

Some examples of nonrecurring expenses include these:

- Moving

- Building repairs and renovations

- Software overhaul

- Legal fees for dispute resolution
- Disaster recovery
- Discontinued business operations
- Insurance payouts
- Gains or losses on asset sales

LENDERS AND ADD-BACKS

There is yet another problem with running personal expenses through your businesses: lenders. The buyer's lender is also interested in your business's profitability. Lenders will account for some add-backs but not to a large extent. The following common items get added back as a matter of course:

- Depreciation
- Amortization
- Interest (sometimes)
  - If you own anything with an industry-specific floor plan, like a car, boat, or motorcycle dealership, interest is a legitimate expense that will be carried over to the new owner.
- Rent (only if the sellers own the real estate and their company pays rent to their real estate holding company)
  - If you own the separate corporation that leases the real estate your business rents, and the business pays that corporation more rent than another tenant would be charged, you can only add back the difference between the "real" rent and what's being paid by the business. For example, if a business paid $150,000 a year in rent to a separate corporation, but the owner is willing to rent the space for $250,000, the difference of $100,000 will be subtracted back. Keep in mind that the $100,000 will decrease the EBITDA, which will decrease the sales price. Many sellers get greedy with rent, and they tend to forget that the more they want to charge the new owner to lease their property, the less they will get paid in the

sale of their business. If the buyer were to buy the building, they'd be buying the equity in the building, and then the entire $250,000 would be added back, thereby increasing the sales price.

THE OWNER'S SALARY

Let's look at how to deal with the owner's salary. If the buyer is not going to run the business, the owner's salary is not added back, because it will be a recurring expense when someone is hired to do the owner's job. If the owner takes $200,000 a year, and the average salary for that position is $75,000, then $125,000 would be added back. Whatever adjustment is made for salary add-backs will affect the EBITDA. In this case, the business will show an increase in cash flow of $125,000, which would increase the sales price.

Salary adjustments are important. For example, if two partners or a married couple pay themselves a total of $300,000 annually to work in the business, don't assume that's an add-back: The buyer can't perform the work of two people, so only the difference between $300,000 and the salary for a second skilled person would get added back. The following chart illustrates some typical add-backs you can use.

It's imperative to know if the owners or partners are needed to stay in the business and at what cost. If you're going to charge the new owner more to stay with the company, this will reduce the cash flow of the business, reducing the sales price. Many owners want us to market the owner's required salary as TBD. The issue with this scenario is, depending on the TBD, it can dramatically affect the selling price.

Seiler Tucker once sold a landscaping company. Three brothers, a sister, and two of the brothers' wives worked in the business. We knew the two brothers (owners) would need to stay on for at least two years. The sister and wives wanted to retire, and they were getting paid more than what a replacement would cost. Therefore, we added back part of their salary and partial benefits, as the two brothers were going to continue the wives' benefits. We did not, however, add back the brothers' salaries and benefits, because they were not willing to work for a reduced rate, even if it were to increase the EBITDA, which increases the sales price.

SAMPLE ADD-BACKS CHART				
	2016	2017	2018	2019
Net income on tax return	1,000,000	1,500,000	2,000,000	2,500,000
Add-backs				
Owner salary	100,000	125,000	200,000	250,000
Personal health insurance	21,000	23,000	25,095	31,500
Personal auto expense car insurance	17,000	20,995	20,500	19,000
Phone and Internet (personal)	8,795	8,500	10,000	9,000
Meals, travel, and entertainment	5,000	7,500	8,000	22,000
Charitable donations	10,000	15,000	25,000	20,000
Country club dues	7,500	7,500	9,500	11,000
Professional fees (personal real estate)	3,300	7,000	10,500	12,000
Nonrecurring (one-time expenses)	5,500	6,500	15,748	12,500
Total add-backs	178,095	220,995	324,343	376,000
Adjusted EBITDA	1,178,095	1,720,995	2,324,343	2,876,000

There are resources we use that determine average salaries for all types of positions in the United States and Canada. Some business owners will pay family members through the business who do not work in the business. This will be an add-back as long as the family member does not contribute to the business or need to be replaced. Remember: If you're going to charge the new owner more to stay with the company, this will reduce the cash flow of the business, thereby reducing the sales price.

CASH

Some businesses prefer to operate in cash. Here's the thing about doing everything in cash: You might save 15 to 25 percent in annual taxes by hiding cash, but it's illegal. On top of the possible criminal consequences, hiding your cash also means you have nothing to show a potential buyer to prove your business is profitable.

While pricing your business depends on how well you're firing on all cylinders and managing the ST 6 P's, it really all comes down to a single P: profits. Buyers need to know your business's value. Without accurate cash flow, you can't price your business appropriately, and that will cost you dearly. If your business is making good profits, we can sell it for a multiple of those earnings. That will far exceed whatever you think you're saving by avoiding taxes.

As an example, the owner of three car and truck accessory retail stores was adamant about selling his business for $1 million. Years of tax returns revealed that, although he was personally making about $65,000 annually, he'd lost money one year and only made a profit of $8,500 the next. He had about $300,000 in inventory and very little in furnishings, fixtures, and equipment. He owned the real estate but wouldn't include it in the deal.

We explained to him there was no way to sell his business for $1 million because there was no money in it (i.e., cash flow to support the asking price). He insisted he was making a lot of money. We told him we couldn't find it and said, "Unless you can show us your cash flow, we can't sell your business for anything close to what you think it should sell for."

After four months of digging through his financials, we were able to prove that he was profiting close to $400,000 every year. The problem was the cash flow that he was reporting. It turned out that he was paying every-thing—employees, contractors, bills—in cash. We told him this was not good business and would affect our ability to market the company. But once we got his finances in order, we were able to sell it for $1.2 million.

No lender would have taken this deal or any deal that looked like it. Our seller had to agree to hold paper on 50 percent of the transaction. Nonetheless, it was a great deal for him. He received $600,000 up front and 7 percent interest on his money for five years. He was also able to keep the real estate and lease all three buildings to the buyer for a profit. Furthermore, he was able to use his leases as additional security on the seller-financing portion.

Once, we were approached by a business owner of a large gymnastics training facility. It was a great business, except for their books and records. Their financials were a complete disaster, so much so that we refused to sell this business until they cleaned their financial house and started reporting all their income. This business had two partners and two bank accounts. One bank account belonged to one partner, who deposited cash and paid per-sonal expenses, while the other account took in reported income. According to them, the personal expenses that they ran through the business were more than the business's gross revenues on paper. They chose to run their company day-to-day, never really planning for the sale of their business. Now that they wanted to sell their business, they needed to focus on fixing the company to operate on the ST 6 P's so the company would be sellable.

Pricing your business depends heavily on a multitude of factors and whether the business operates on all the ST 6 P's. However, it also comes down to the facts. Buyers will look under the hood and want to test drive your baby so they can understand what you are truly making in your business.

If your business does not show a healthy profit (most don't) on its tax returns, it is almost impossible to sell the business without determining your add-backs. This process can get very complicated, and it is difficult to accomplish on your own. Many business owners have been living out of their business for so long that they truly are clueless when it comes to knowing their add-backs. You can maximize your value if you use the assis-tance of a professional, experienced M&A advisor or business broker to peel back all the layers of the onion to uncover your SDE (seller's discretionary earnings). Without identifying your SDE, you do not know what your business is truly worth.

MENTORING CORNER

The more data you have organized for the buyer, including the add-backs or adjustments described in this chapter, the easier due diligence will be for you. It also shows your willingness to be open and transparent to your potential buyer. In preparation for selling, you will want to have your financial statements ready. Be sure to have your accountants provide the backup for the financials as well. Buyers will also want to see your tax returns so they can compare them to the financial statements.

Serious buyers will most likely take it a step further and ask to see your bank statements. They may even have their accountants try to match your bank statement activity to your financial statements and possibly trace the activity back to invoices or receipts.

Even when you can prove actual numbers, inadequacies in record keeping can have consequences with prospective buyers. Some may simply be scared off with the potential of tax or other liabilities and insist on significant holdbacks or reserves against such liabilities. Others may insist on structuring the deal as an asset purchase rather than acquisition of the entity, minimizing the value of goodwill of the entity and potentially decreasing the sales price.

 KNOW MORE TO EXIT RICH

In this chapter, we talked about how to organize your financial data to help you prepare your business for sale. The better organized you are, the easier the selling and due diligence process will be for you. The more open and transparent you are with the buyer, the more comfortable they will feel with the overall transaction, making them less likely to back out of a deal. Make sure your financials are in order now so that when it comes time to sell, you can present your company in the best possible light, which will work in your favor at the negotiating table.

DID YOU KNOW?

- According to Oxfam America, US corporations are reportedly hiding $1.6 trillion in profits offshore.

- Abrigo states that 50 to 80 percent of a small business owner's net worth is tied into the business.

- According to Fox Business, entrepreneurs, on average, pay themselves $68,000 a year.

- According to *Entrepreneur*, loading your business with tax write-offs can make you appear less profitable and may cause a buyer to under-value your business.

IMPLEMENTATION IS KEY

To further explore the lessons learned in this chapter, implement the following:

- Prepare all your financial records.
- Report all your income.
- Do the add-back exercise to determine your SDE/EBITDA.
- Be sure to add back all nonrecurring expenses.
- Make sure you can prove all of your add-backs to a buyer.

To watch a free video of Michelle explaining addbacks and non-reoccurring expenses called "How Many Owners Are Unaware of Their Actual Cash Flow and EBITDA," please visit SeilerTuckerAcademy.com.

12

Determining What Your Business Is Really Worth Using the ST 6 P Method®

"Price is what you pay. Value is what you get."

—Warren Buffett

Your business is worth whatever a buyer is willing to pay for it. All you need to arrive at that number are the ST 6 P's. Businesses sell for maximum value when they're running on all ST 6 P's. When a buyer comes around to check under the hood and kick the tires of your company, they'll be driving it right off the lot. But let us tell you from personal experience, it's easy to have a blind spot and a prejudice where your baby is concerned. Business owners are like parents; all parents think their child is the best looking, smartest, and funniest. Business owners think the same way about their businesses; their baby is the best and should demand the highest price. The hardest part of our job, however, is telling owners their baby is not as pretty as they think. Unfortunately, in most cases, their business will not demand maximum value, because they are not operating on all the ST 6 P's, and the business is not making enough money to support their dream price.

To sell your business at the highest price, you must inspect every one of your P's (people, product, process, proprietary, patrons, and profits) to see where you are right now and how you could grow your business by improving the performance of one or more of the P's. Bringing in experts to help in that assessment can be invaluable.

How do you go about making sure you've uncovered, revealed, and examined everything about your business so you are satisfied there will be no surprises or money left on the table? To sell your business, you will need to get your business valuated. To do this, you will need to prepare and provide all financials. (Our firm has compiled a comprehensive list of the financial forms and reports that are needed to evaluate the worth of your business, found on the next page.) You will also need to provide all the financial records to the buyer (found on the next page), the buyer's CPA, and lender upon their request. If you engage an M&A advisor or business broker, you need to provide these documents to your advisory team first. Your representative will then distribute documents as needed to the buyer and their professional team. Our firm typically puts together a confidential information memorandum (CIM) that includes a three- to five-year financial spreadsheet highlighting add-backs. We will not give our seller's tax returns and other proprietary documents to buyers and their team without a written and an executed purchase offer agreement or LOI with appropriate confidentiality provisions and escrow money.

DOCUMENTS SELLERS MUST PROVIDE

Sellers must provide prospective buyers with three to five years of the following documents:

- Tax returns
- Profit and loss (P&L) statements from previous years
- Current P&Ls
- Cash flow statements
- Bank statements (if applicable)
- Annual balance sheets from previous years
- Current balance sheets
- W-2s for all owners and family members
- An accounts receivable report
- An accounts payable report
- A work-in-process report
- Projections
- An FF&E list (furniture, fixtures, and equipment)
- Inventory
- A list of all debts and creditors
- An appraisal (if applicable)
- A lease (if applicable)
- A franchise agreement (if applicable)
- A list of demonstrable intellectual property assets—patents, trademark registrations, copyright registrations
- A list of significant contracts

Sellers must be able to prove what expenses they are running through the business. The list of common and uncommon add-backs in golden nugget 11 will help you with this process.

A CURRENT FF&E LIST

A business's FF&E contributes to its value; therefore, you need to have a current FF&E list so buyers know what physical assets they're buying. Companies—especially large manufacturing, trucking, and construction companies—may have to obtain an FF&E appraisal. FF&E certainly adds value to the sale of your business. However, if you are upside down in FF&E and the cash flow does not support the price tag on your FF&E, you might not be able to recoup your investment.

For example, we met with a chemical manufacturing owner. The sellers wanted $3,200,000 for their business, because that was the value of their FF&E and inventory. However, they were still carrying the debt for the FF&E and inventory, so the actual contribution of the inventory toward the value of business was $3,200,000 less the debt.

It turns out their cash flow was only about $100,000 per year. This meant they were upside down in FF&E and inventory. Because of this, the cash flow did not come anywhere close to supporting their asking price. My sellers were unreasonable and not coachable. They insisted on an unrealistic selling price and are now out of business and filing for bankruptcy.

An FF&E list can be difficult to keep up-to-date, because owners are constantly adding and replacing new furniture, fixtures, and equipment on top of throwing things away. Should you change FF&E after you put your company up for sale, update the list and notify your M&A advisor or business broker. Buyers have the right to walk through your business a few days prior to closing to inspect all FF&E on the list. If something is wrong, you need to fix it or replace it before closing or make appropriate concessions.

Also, be sure to include the manufacturer (if applicable), the serial number (if applicable), the VIN number (if you have vehicles or heavy equipment), and the year and make of vehicles included. Make sure you include quantities of tables, chairs, and other furniture.

INCLUDED AND NOT-INCLUDED LISTS

On another occasion, we were working with a seller that had a multimillion-dollar business. When the attorneys were going through the closing documents, they started discussing the list of FF&E that was to be included in the sale.

The buyer mentioned that the large flat-screen television located in the seller's conference room was not on the list and needed to be added. "The TV is not included," the business owner said. "I'm taking it home."

The buyer was furious. "This is ridiculous after all the money I am spending on this business," he said. "The TV had better be included, or I am not purchasing your business."

The seller's attorney said that the TV was marked on the not-included list, so all parties reviewed the not-included list. And you know what they found? The flat-screen TV was *not* listed; in fact, it was not on the included list either.

The buyer and seller began arguing again. The seller was making a fortune on the sale of his business, so he could have easily included the TV. The buyer was spending millions on the business, and in the big picture spending another thousand dollars on a television was not much to add to the bill. Nevertheless, neither side was budging.

Michelle jumped up from where she was sitting at the conference-room table. "Everyone calm down," she said. "I will buy another flat-screen TV for the conference room."

That very day, she went to the store, purchased a TV, and gave it to the buyer. In the end, everyone was happy, and the deal closed.

The moral of the story is to make sure that if you are *not* including something, you record it on the not-included list. If you have a Mercedes that you pay for through the business but you are not including it in the sale of the business, you must record this car on the not-included list. It is very important to have an included list and a not-included list and to double-check each list to avoid squabbles during closing.

INVENTORY

If a business has a large inventory, an inventory report is critical to pricing the business, because its value is included. Inventory is included in the sale of the business at cost, not retail.

We track first-in-first-out (FIFO) and last-in-first-out (LIFO) inventory as a way of examining how finances are tied up in a company. Briefly, FIFO indicates that the oldest inventory items are sold first, and LIFO means that the most recently produced items are recorded as sold first.

At closing, the value of the inventory is usually adjusted upward or downward, depending on an inventory count conducted one to three days before closing. Inventory count is taken in one of several ways. If it's a small business, the buyer and seller can agree to take inventory together. Medium to larger companies may require the assistance of a third-party inventory company, with the fee usually split between buyer and seller.

Keep in mind that the buyer will walk through your business prior to closing to value the inventory and determine if the sales price should be adjusted up or down. We once sold a company that specializes in oil field rental, sale, and service. Their inventory was valued at several million dollars and was a key part of the business, since it generated the company's revenues. Because it was so integral to the sale, the inventory had to be valued by a third party before finalizing the valuation of the business to maximize value.

SELLER ACCOUNTS RECEIVABLE

Expert M&A advisors and business brokers assign a value (based on your collection history) to accounts receivable. In most cases, this will increase the value of your business. Your company may not have current accounts receivable; many small businesses won't, whereas medium to large businesses will. Some buyers won't buy a business without current accounts receivable, while others feel they won't be able to collect the accounts receivable, so they don't want them included in the sales price.

Nevertheless, a business's average monthly accounts receivable and average monthly collection rate can be negotiating tools, and the industry will dictate how the accounts receivable gets treated in the sale of a business.

For example, we are selling a chiropractic clinic. This clinic specializes in personal injury and takes most patients on contingency. It's typical for them to have millions in receivables. However, this clinic collects about 60 to 70 percent of their accounts receivable, and it could take years to collect. The business does not have enough cash flow to justify millions of dollars for its receivables up front. Therefore, we market this business with a certain amount of accounts receivable included. The remainder will be paid as collected: 60 percent to the new owner and 40 percent to the previous owner. The reason the new owner gets more accounts receivable upon collection is because they are collecting the receivables, keeping the clients happy, and they need the accounts receivable for working capital, since most of the cash flow is contingent on collecting the receivables.

ACCOUNTS PAYABLE

Many sellers feel that if the buyer retains the accounts receivable, they should also be responsible for the accounts payable. Whether a buyer is responsible for accounts payable depends on whether those receivables are associated with the payables and, ultimately, on what's negotiated.

THE TWO TYPES OF SALES

There are two types of business sales: asset sales and stock sales. In this next section, we will explore both types of sales to help you differentiate between the two.

ASSET SALES

Asset sales can be used to sell any type of business and include the sale of the various assets that a business may own. Assets may be tangible or intangible, with tangible assets including land, buildings, equipment, cash, investments, and inventory and intangible assets being the business's reputation, customer lists, patents, copyrights, and trademarks.

Within an asset sale, there is a degree of choice when deciding what you are selling, because you may reserve the right to keep a specific asset associated with the business. In an asset sale, the buyer is buying the assets of your company, and those assets will need to be free and clear of all liens and encumbrances at closing.

All debt will have to be paid at closing, including loans, lines of credit, equipment and vehicle leases, and payables, if they are associated with collected receivables. This can sometimes get complicated and muddy the water, depending on the industry and the buyer's terms.

When our firm sold the aforementioned multimillion-dollar oil field business, the company was an asset sale and had two divisions, one on shore and the other off. The buyer's LOI required that all payables be paid off at closing by the seller. The payables also included paying off all inventory ordered for completed and uncompleted jobs if the inventory was in the company's warehouse or located at the jobsite. However, if the inventory was in the middle of the ocean en route to the business or jobsite, it would be paid for by the buyer. The buyer did not care if the outstanding payables were associated with future, uncollected accounts receivable. The seller disliked the terms and countered the buyer's offer, stating, "Accounts payable associated with future uncollected accounts receivable would be paid by the buyer." The buyer rejected the counter, ready to move on to the next possible acquisition. The seller liked all other terms and conditions and, therefore, ended up accepting the buyer's offer. Please note, this is the exception rather than the rule; most accounts payable associated with accounts receivable is paid by the buyer if the buyer is buying the accounts receivable. However, he who holds the gold makes the rules, showing us that everything is negotiable. The seller still profited hugely from the sale of their business, despite those specific unfavorable terms.

STOCK SALES

When a buyer purchases the selling shareholders' stock or equity interest directly, it is done so through a stock stale. Stock sales mean the seller is selling the business entity, where the assets and liabilities are held within the entity. However, contrary to an asset sale, stock sales do not require multiple separate conveyances of each individual asset. This is because the title of each asset lies within the corporation. According to an analysis on marketplace transactions from the Pratt's Stats database, about 30 percent of all transactions are stock sales. Larger transactions have a greater likelihood of being stock sales.

When dealing with stock sales, buyers lose the ability to redepreciate specific assets. Buyers run a higher risk when buying a company's stock due to unknown risk of future lawsuits, environmental concerns, OSHA violations, employee issues, and other liabilities. The buyer may have recourse against the seller by reason of breach of representations and warranties and, sometimes, indemnity provisions in the stock purchase agreement.

Sellers often prefer stock sales, because all proceeds are taxed according to a lower capital gains rate, and in C corporations, the corporate level taxes are bypassed. Similar risks for future liabilities, such as product liability claims, contract claims, employee lawsuits, and pensions, are often taken into account by sellers.

WORKING CAPITAL

Working capital, also known as net working capital, is an accounting term that refers to a company's available capital for daily operations at any given point in time. It is the difference between a company's current assets, such as cash, customers' unpaid bills, inventories of raw materials and finished goods, and its current liabilities. A key part of financial modeling involves forecasting a balance sheet. Working capital refers to the specific subset of balance sheet items. For a company to operate effectively, it should have more assets than liabilities to ensure success in paying back any long-term debt. The amount of working capital a company has is a good indicator of its liquidity, efficiency, and financial health.

A working capital ratio (comparing assets to liabilities) value of 1.2 to 2.0 indicates a good working capital. A ratio less than 1.0 indicates negative working capital, showing potential for liquidity problems, whereas a ratio above 2.0 serves as an indicator that the company is not using its extra assets to produce maximum possible revenue. A company with negative working capital is commonly addressed as being in financial risk. A company with working capital is seen as being in decent short-term financial health. Even with a significant amount of positive working capital, a company can experience a shortage in cash if its current assets are not able to be liquidated quickly.

Working capital is also a negotiating tool. There are many different formulas to calculate it. The amount of working capital required depends on the type of business and the type of buyer. Buyers buying multimillion-dollar businesses will require that working capital be included in the sale.

There are different ways of calculating working capital, and buyers will define their working capital differently. We once sold a $15 million manufacturing company as an asset sale. The buyers used a formula of twelve months trailing financials to calculate the working capital. They then specified the amount of accounts receivable and inventory to be included in the sales price of the business. If the agreed-upon receivables or inventory amount decreased, the sales price would decrease. No matter how many times we explained this concept to our owners, they decided not to comply with the terms of the agreement. They insisted on collecting as much accounts receivable as possible before the closing so they could pocket the money. By doing so, they ended up receiving less at the closing table. Therefore, keep in mind that if you are going to collect accounts receivable or sell off inventory, you should expect a lower selling price.

LENDER OR SMALL BUSINESS ASSOCIATION FINANCING REQUIREMENT

Whether it's an asset or a stock sale, the debt and line of credit (LOC) must be paid off at closing, because all liens and encumbrances must be removed before the lender funds. Sometimes, the buyer and seller will implement a cutoff date for accounts receivable and accounts payable before closing. This can become complicated, so we recommend that you use a professional to navigate through all the legalities.

REAL ESTATE AND LEASES

If real estate is part of the sale of your business, you need to have a recent real estate appraisal. This small investment will pay off immensely in the valuation of your business.

If you lease space for your business, the advisor or broker and the buyer need to see that it's solid and long term. It's beneficial if it's transferable or you can sublease.

There's a real danger in a month-to-month lease. Buyers are not always interested in an existing business; sometimes they're more interested in your location.

ENVIRONMENTAL ISSUES

If there are environmental issues that affect your business, you must let the buyer know. These could be health issues that affect employees, such as contaminated drinking water, or there could be waste disposal issues that involve necessary permits and inspections.

As you can see, this comprehensive list of needed information will uncover every detail that's relevant to your business and determining its value. Obviously, you want to have all this information in hand well before you offer your business for sale, because it all contributes to pricing your company for maximum value at sale. Don't worry if you can't figure out how it all comes together to establish that figure: That's what your M&A advisor or business broker is for.

There is no one size that fits all when determining what a business is worth. We certainly do not want to point fingers at any one profession. However, my sellers have told me horrific stories about what "outside professionals" claimed their business was worth. We have heard different formulas that make absolutely no sense, such as five times gross income. No one is going to pay you five times gross for your business. It does not make sense and will never meet the Buyer's Sanity Check. We have also had sellers who were very upset because these same professionals charged them $15,000 to $20,000 to evaluate their business.

When sellers engage our firm to sell their business for the amount that these professionals have valued their business for, we must start from scratch and revalue the seller's business to make sure the seller is getting the highest selling price possible. Our experience has shown that, in most cases, the valuation of the business provided to us was way too much—or, even worse, way too low.

We once worked with a physical therapy company that wanted to sell their business. The partners had paid their CPA $17,000 to value their business. He valued their business for approximately $600,000. Even though he was a CPA, he did not pull industry standards or business comps or back into the cash flow to ensure the business cash flows were enough to support a $600,000 asking price. In addition, he did not valuate the company operations.

When we take engagements, we don't price businesses based on the valuation of third parties, nor do we base our valuation on what the seller wants for their business. We run the numbers, do projections via the discounted cash flow method, value intangible assets, pull industry standards, and pull business comps. We also look at all the other characteristics (the ST 6 P's) of the business before pricing it.

Unfortunately, we did not come up with a price tag of $600,000. That number did not compute. They had only been in business for three years and were making a little over $100,000 a year, including add-backs. They were operating on three of the ST 6 P's, not six. Upon completing our valuation, we told them that their business was worth $430,000. Needless to say, they were shocked, devastated, and upset that our valuation was so much lower than their CPA's valuation. To validate the price, we showed them industry standards and business comps, and, most important, we backed into their cash flow and demonstrated how the CPA's $600,000 price tag did not meet the Buyer's Sanity Check. The cash flow would not service the buyer's debt or leave the buyer with enough money to live on, and it would not provide the buyer a return on their investment for years to come, if ever. We explained that if the Buyer's Sanity Check was not met, no one would buy their business. When we explained my valuation to the partners, they completely understood and were furious that they had paid their CPA $17,000 to give them an unrealistic price on their business. We marketed their business for $430,000 and received an offer for $460,000. We were able to sell their business for the highest maximum value in thirty days.

FIVE PRIMARY TYPES OF VALUATION METHODS

When deciding to sell your business, it's important to understand what your business is worth. There are five primary types of valuation methods. For the best and most accurate results, we compare two or more methods. The following business valuation methods will assist you in figuring out your business's value:

ASSET

Your company's assets include tangible and intangible items. Use the book or market value of those assets to determine your business's worth. Count all the cash, equipment, inventory, real estate, stocks, options, patents, trademarks, and customer relationships as you calculate the asset valuation for your business.

HISTORICAL EARNINGS

A business's gross income, ability to repay debt, and capitalization of cash flow or earnings determine its current value. If your business struggles to bring in enough income to pay bills, its value drops. Conversely, repaying debt quickly and maintaining a positive cash flow improves your business's value. Use all of these factors as you determine your business's historical earnings valuation.

RELATIVE

With the relative valuation method, you determine how much similar businesses would bring if they were sold. It compares the value of your business's assets to the value of similar assets and gives you a reasonable asking price.

FUTURE MAINTAINABLE EARNINGS

The profitability of your business in the future determines its value today, and you can use the future maintainable earnings valuation method for business valuation when profits are expected to remain stable. To calculate your business's future maintainable earnings valuation, evaluate its sales, expenses, profits, and gross profits from the past three years. These figures help you predict the future and give your business a value today.

DISCOUNT CASH FLOW

If profits are not expected to remain stable in the future, use the discount cash flow valuation method. It takes your business's future net cash flows and discounts them to present-day values. With those figures, you know the discounted cash flow valuation of your business and how much money your business assets are expected to make in the future.

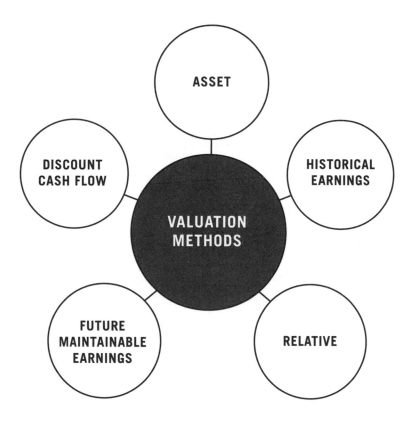

DIFFERENT TYPES OF FORMULAS USED

In addition to the valuation method that you choose, there are different types of formulas used to determine the value of your business. They are as follows:

A PERCENTAGE OF GROSS INCOME

The first method is to use a percentage of the total gross income of your business. However, you should not include unrelated business income in your gross income. Some examples include other rental income that is not included in the sale of your business or insurance claims related to disaster recoveries or other one-time occurrences. This income is not the norm and should not be used in the valuation of your business.

A MULTIPLE OF ADJUSTED EBITDA

EBITDA is the earnings before interest, taxes, depreciation, and amortization on your business. This formula is typically used in larger businesses that have a lot of assets to depreciate. Depreciation and amortization are nonexpense items on the tax return and do not affect cash flow on the P&L. It is common practice to add back interest and taxes, because the new owner's interest and taxes will be different from the previous owner's. In this formula, we also take into consideration the owner's personal and nonrecurring expenses.

A MULTIPLE OF EBIT

EBIT is your earnings before interest and taxes. Some examples include businesses that are light in assets and will not have much depreciation and amortization, such as photography, appraisers, and insurance adjusters. Again, we add back the taxes and interest due to the new owners being different upon purchase.

A MULTIPLE OF SDE

SDE is the seller's discretionary earnings. The seller's discretionary earnings take into consideration all the owner's personal and nonrecurring expenses. This formula is typically for smaller businesses that don't have a lot of assets to depreciate.

A MULTIPLE OF NET INCOME

You can use the net income or loss that appears on your tax returns to value your business. Some industry standards base the value on the business's net income on the tax returns. This formula is the least likely to be used, because most businesses will have personal or nonrecurring expenses, depreciation, amortization, interest, and taxes.

Again, there is not a one-size-fits-all formula. Many industries use several formulas to determine the selling price. The best practice is to evaluate each formula associated with industry standards and business comparables to determine which formula will maximize the value of your business.

When allocating a purchase price on your business, you must take into consideration whether the business operates on all six cylinders, the 6 P Method. The more cylinders the business operates on, the higher the multiple and the higher the price the business will demand.

Refresh yourself on the ST 6 P's and what drives value. There are always components in a business that add or subtract value. When evaluating a business for sale, we absolutely take everything into consideration so we can, in most cases, sell our client's business for more than it is worth in the quickest possible amount of time.

The items listed above should and will be considered in pricing your business for sale. Some business owners have unrealistic expectations, whereas others significantly undervalue their business. Which type of seller are you?

THE BUYER'S SANITY CHECK

As we discovered, there are five types of buyers. No matter what type of buyer you're selling your company to, they all ask five basic questions to ensure that your company meets their Buyer's Sanity Check. The most important thing you need to know is that the price of your business must meet the Buyer's Sanity Check or no one will buy, leaving your business to sit on the market for years and potentially never sell. To avoid this scenario, familiarize yourself with the following:

THE BUYER'S SANITY CHECK

- How much money do I have to put down on this business?
- Will the cash flow of the business support the debt service?
- After the debt service is paid, how much money is left to live on?
- How soon can I get an ROI?
- Does the business have potential to grow?

Buyers will not pay for potential; however, they will not buy a business unless it has potential. Buyers are not going to pay twice. It takes money, time, energy, and effort to grow a business to the next level; therefore, buyers are not going to want to pay a seller for potential and then pay more money to realize that potential.

Most buyers will not buy a business if they cannot receive positive answers to the Buyer's Sanity Check questions listed above. In addition, most buyers will want to recoup their initial investment within two to three years. Therefore, if the price tag on your business does not line up with the Buyer's Sanity Check, your price does not make sense and will not appeal to buyers, unless it's a strategic or competitive buyer buying synergies.

When selling your business, ask yourself: Do you want to ask a high price for your business even if your adjusted EBITDA does not support it? Or do you want your business to sell? There are thousands of businesses that have been sitting on the market for years that will never sell because they are overpriced. The right M&A advisor or business broker can help steer you through the pricing process so you can sell your business at a fair and profitable price.

We once had a motorcycle dealership that wanted us to value their business. It was listed with a business broker for three years at $7 million. We asked the seller who came up with that price tag—him or the broker? The seller replied, "I did." We then asked him whether the broker performed a valuation and pulled industry standards and business comps and whether they analyzed them to see if his business ran on all six cylinders? He replied, "NO!"

We pulled up his listing and discovered that the business had been reduced to $5 million. We then asked him if the business broker valued his company to come up with a more realistic price or if something had changed in his business to lower the price by $2 million. He replied, "Nothing changed to lower my price. I was not getting any interested buyers, so I called the broker and had him lower the price." His broker was merely an order taker, not a professional M&A advisor or business broker. He had been in business brokering for many years; however, he did nothing whatsoever to valuate and sell the seller's business. Unfortunately, many advisors and brokers are order takers instead of experts.

Soon afterward, we met with the seller and performed an extensive valuation on his business. His business was not worth $7 million or even $5 million. It was worth $3.8 million. However, because the company had sat on the market for so many years without any interest, the business started trending downward, particularly because of changes in the economy, the owner's age, and the business's lack of innovation and marketing. Unfortunately, the business never sold, because the seller was unrealistic, waited too long, and had initially hired the wrong brokerage firm.

WHEN NOT TO SET A PRICE

In many instances, we do not put a price on the business when we go to market. The reason we do this is that if the business operates on all the ST 6 P's and has over a million dollars in EBITDA, we know we will have hundreds of buyers for that business, thus creating a bidding war. This happens because there are more buyers for great businesses with high cash flow than there are buyers for small, struggling businesses. Remember: Buyers for struggling businesses tend to be strategic buyers; they do not just buy based on EBITDA. They are also buying synergies. Therefore, they are willing to pay for something they currently don't have, such as people, clients, and congruent revenue streams, and, in many cases, they are willing to pay top dollar and outbid their competitors. They are also willing to take a calculated risk to catapult their business to the next level. That's why it's so imperative to study this blueprint and to build your business using the ST 6 P's and to increase profits so your business will be considered by hundreds of buyers that are willing to outbid everyone else.

CASE STUDY

ENERGY COMPANY

The company we will look at is actually composed of two companies: one thriving, the other teetering on failure.

OPERATED ON MOST OF THE ST 6 P'S

- People: The company had tenured employees and a management team in place.
- Product: Their product was proprietary and in demand, with little to no competition. However, they were in the oil industry, which is extremely volatile, and was plummeting at the time.
- Process: They were efficient and well documented.
- Proprietary: They had eighteen patents and master service agreements in place that were transferable.
- Patrons: They had a diversified clientele in the US and several other countries.
- Profits: The business was producing a little over $2 million in EBITDA. The company also had extensive accounts receivable.
- Appraised value: $8.4 million

BUYERS' AND SELLERS' PAIN POINTS

- The oil industry was plummeting.
- The second company was upside down in inventory and accounts payable, and it was headed into foreclosure.
- The seller's ex-partner, brother, and son were being very difficult to deal with and were not acting in good faith.
- The seller was going through a complicated, nasty divorce.

OUTCOME

- Successful marketing efforts to private equity groups, strategic buyers and competitors, and sophisticated buyers.

- Over 550 buyers were looking at this business during the oil bust.

- Seiler Tucker created a bidding war and received several LOIs within weeks of seller engagement.

- Negotiated the buyer up to $5.5 million from an initial bid of $7.5 million including the sale of the seller's second company, for a grand total of $13 million for 80 percent of the company.

- Negotiated the owner's salary, plus benefits, plus equity.

THE STORY

This oil-manufacturing business was actually two companies: one offshore, one onshore. The offshore company was quite successful, even during a time when oil prices were plummeting. The onshore business was struggling for a multitude of reasons. The business structure was complicated. For example, the seller's ex-partner in the business owned the real estate. Things were made difficult because the ex-partner was not negotiating in good faith.

During the selling process, the owners did not always listen to the advice we gave them. For example, we inform all sellers and potential sellers not to tell employees, clients, and vendors that the owners are selling their business. Despite this, the seller told their employees, resulting in one key employee demanding more compensation to stay and another one deciding to leave. Other potential problems arose due to breach of confidentiality.

Nevertheless, many buyers saw the potential in the business, and several buyers wanted to bid on it. The key was to price and package the business correctly. The deal involved a series of complicated negotiations with the buyers and sellers, uncovering losses, ensuring that payables were paid, and dealing with personnel problems. However, in the end, because this business was running on all ST 6 P's we were able to create a bidding war, and the business was successfully sold.

SAMPLE VALUATION ST 6 P'S SCORES

PEOPLE   4.00

This business has employees and some management in place. The owner is still involved, but most likely working on the business, not in the day-to-day operations.

PRODUCT   2.00

The product/business is in a volatile industry, however the owner is innovating, diversifying, and marketing.

PROCESS   3.00

The business has great processes, but lacks documentation and employee training.

PROPRIETARY   5.00

The business operates on all proprietary levels: well branded, been in business for many years, great brand awareness and brand recognition. They have brand advocacy, a database, transferable contracts, patents, trade secrets, and trademarks.

PATRONS   5.00

The business has customers in one or two specific areas, such as age, gender, etc. They are not diversified and are at risk of losing their market share and may end up going out of business.

PROFITS   5.00

The business is extremely profitable and has $1 million+ in EBITDA.

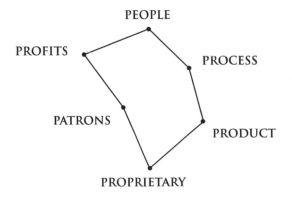

We persevered through all the challenges and engaged legal or accounting experts in both transactions to facilitate due diligence, prepare the closing documents, and reduce the seller's tax liability. We can typically obtain a 20 to 40 percent higher selling price than our seller's business appraises for. However, in some cases, we have been able to obtain a 50 to 65 percent higher selling price (premium) for 70 to 80 percent of the business.

While the sales price is important, what's more important is what you walk away with at the end of the sale. All sellers must, therefore, answer an important question: Do you want a high price for your business, or do you want it to sell for maximum value in the quickest time possible? There is a big difference between hiring a professional, experienced M&A advisor or business broker and hiring a order taker. In the appendix (bonus nugget 3), we share how to properly interview and hire an experienced M&A advisor or business broker so that you can walk away with the most profit possible on the sale of your business. The key is to price and package your business correctly. Most important, it's imperative to build your business to run on all the ST 6 P's and create a bidding war to obtain the highest price.

MENTORING CORNER

You have heard the phrase "penny wise, pound foolish." This chapter proves the need for professional assistance in selling your business. Having an experienced broker or advisor will ensure that all aspects of the sale are addressed and that you are receiving the highest value for your business. Yes, their fees may be higher than less experienced alternatives, but when they add millions to your final sales price—and, therefore, millions to your pocket, you will be happy to pay them.

For instance, one client Sharon was mentoring was selling their construction business, which included millions of dollars' worth of equipment like bulldozers, cranes, and other equipment as part of its FF&E. As it happened, the book value of the equipment was quite low because it had been almost entirely written off through depreciation over the last few years. However, the equipment was clearly still valuable. Although both the buyer and the seller recognized that the equipment was valuable, they were both surprised when the broker's appraiser validated a significantly higher value

continued

for the equipment. In fact, the equipment was valued at $2 million more than expected. And through the process, the broker even helped find a buyer, another client, for some of the equipment that the buyer was not interested in acquiring.

An experienced broker will also be able to review the pros and cons of an asset sale of your company versus a stock or equity sale. For instance, an asset sale reduces the risk of potential liabilities being passed from the seller to the buyer, whereas an equity deal may avoid triggering antiassignment provisions in contracts.

The negotiation and due diligence process holds no mystery for an experienced advisor or broker. They know what is reasonable in connection with that process and what is not. They can temper unrealistic expectations. They also know where to look for and present value in your company. Not only will having the right advisor or broker to guide you through the process of selling your business make you significantly more money, it will also reduce the drama and day-to-day stress of the selling process.

KNOW MORE TO EXIT RICH

In this chapter, we learned how to determine what your business is worth to a buyer by looking at the ST 6 P's: people, product, process, proprietary, patrons, and profits. As we discussed earlier in the book, your business will be worth a lot more to a buyer if it is running smoothly on all ST 6 P's. Bringing in an expert to help you inspect each one of your P's will prove invaluable. With their guidance, you will be able to see where you are right now and how you can make your business more attractive to buyers by improving the performance of one or more of these P's.

DID YOU KNOW?

- Twenty percent of busted deals for business brokers and bankers are due to a gap in pricing between buyers and sellers.

- According to *Forbes*, two-thirds of sellers agreed that "getting full value for [their] business to fund retirement or other business interests" was their top goal in the transition of the business, but less than 40 percent had a formal valuation conducted in the last three years, and 65 percent have never had their financial statements audited.

- According to *Wealth Management Magazine*, in 2013, 12 million boomer business owners were getting ready to retire and flood the market with businesses for sale. Five years later, however, only 25 percent of companies actually sold at asking price.

IMPLEMENTATION IS KEY

To further explore the lessons learned in this chapter, implement the following:

- Gather all required financial documents.
- Have your company evaluated using the 6 P Method.
- Tune up your weakest P's.
- When ready, hire an experienced M&A advisor or business broker to create a bidding war on your business.

> To watch a free video by Michelle outlining the steps she takes to evaluate a business, please visit SeilerTuckerAcademy.com.

ST 6 P QUIZ

Score your business from 1–5 on each of the P's
1 being the worst and 5 being the best

PEOPLE   _____

PRODUCT   _____

PROCESS   _____

PROPRIETARY   _____

PATRONS   _____

PROFITS   _____

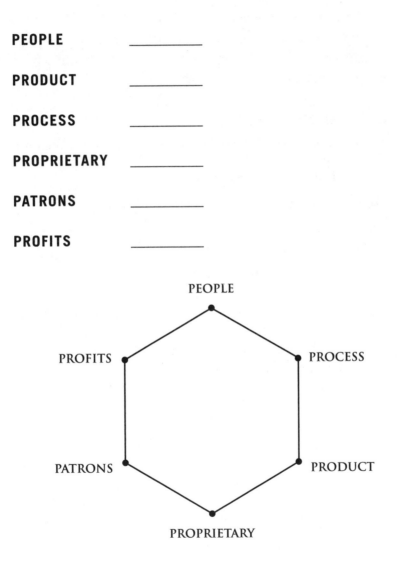

Stage Your Business for Sale

"Never underestimate the power of curb appeal;
remember, people always go where the grass is greener."
—Darla McConnell

In most cases, selling your business will be one of the most important decisions you will ever make, and your business will be the most valuable thing you will ever sell in your lifetime. We discussed financial housekeeping in the previous chapter. In most cases, buyers will see the financials and marketing materials before they visit your business. In other situations, buyers will look at the business first before reviewing the financials. Either way, to obtain maximum value, it is imperative that you clean your business from top to bottom, inside and out.

When selling a house, you or your real estate agent will usually stage the house for sale. They will tell you to start with the outside and work your way in, cleaning the exterior and removing clutter and oversized furniture in the interior. Less is more when showing a house. The same is true for your business. Buyers will judge your business by what they see on the outside long before walking into your business. Granted, you do not have to go through the same extent you would when staging a house for sale. You are not going to redo cabinets, flooring, and decorate the place so it looks like no one works there. However, you will have to look at your business and its surroundings through the buyer's eyes.

Whether your business is large, medium, or small, buyers are going to judge your location, the visibility of your signage, and the curb appeal. They are going to determine if they think the business is busy or slow, if the owner runs a tight ship, if the employees are dressed professionally, if the staff is courteous, and so on.

It is obviously easier to stage a house than a business. Let's face it: We seem to live in our business more than our home. In addition, the employees do not know the business is for sale, so it's not like you can tell them to start wearing uniforms. However, you should enlist the employees to help you clean up shop. They do not need to know you are selling in order to clean up the business and remove clutter.

Over the years of selling businesses, we have seen it all, whether the business is a small café or a multimillion-dollar medical staffing company. We have walked into businesses that were so filthy, dusty, and full of animal hair that we could not breathe. In these instances, we literally had to meet the sellers outside or have them come to our office. If you cannot walk into a business because you get sick from the dust and dirt, what do you think a buyer is going to do? They, too, will walk in and walk out, without any further consideration of buying the business. Many businesses are on the market today. It is a competitive industry; when you put your business on the market, you are competing with thousands of other businesses and franchises for sale. If you want to maximize value when selling your company, you need to make your business shine above all others.

For example, we went to meet with a B&B (bed and breakfast) owner whose business was for sale. It was in a fantastic location, and the property was quaint and charming. The owners had canceled our engagement meeting four times because they were always sick. For the life of us, we could not fig-ure out what was wrong with them. Finally, one day, they decided to honor their commitment and meet with us. The minute we walked in, we realized why they were always so sick. This B&B should have been on the hit show *Hoarders*! The sellers had all kinds of—in our eyes—junk everywhere on the property. Papers, furnishings, and other items were stacked from floor to ceil-ing. Everything was filthy and dusty. They were sick because they had aller-gies caused by dust mites.

It was a beautiful, charming B&B; however, we could not show it to our buyers, because you could barely see the walls, floors, or ceilings. We asked the sellers to go through every room and decide what was staying and what was going. We recommended that they remove 50 percent of the furnishings, decorations, antiques, and junk. They said they would, but of course they did not. We showed the business to prospective buyers numerous times. However, the potential buyers couldn't seem to get past the obvious clutter to realize the potential of this charming B&B.

Learn from this example. Do not be lazy when selling your business. Instead, do whatever it takes to earn your big payday. We could have sold this B&B for millions, including the real estate. To this day, unfortunately, they have not lifted one finger to clean house, and they are still always sick! As a result, we stopped bringing buyers to see the property until they could take control of their business and life and hire a cleaning or trash removal com-pany to remove the clutter to make their B&B look better.

KEY ELEMENTS BUYERS LOOK AT WHEN VISITING YOUR BUSINESS

There are several key elements that buyers will look at and use to form their own perception when visiting your business. Keep in mind that a buyer's per-ception becomes your reality. Therefore, it is in your best interest to be proac-tive and to create positive perceptions. If you are going to lose a buyer, don't lose them because of how the business looks. The better your business looks on the outside, the more peace of mind the buyers will have that you must be properly managing the business. Let's face it: We live in a very judgmental society. Therefore, if you follow the tips in this book, you will only leave buyers with the perception of wanting to know more, see more, and, most importantly, pay more.

Following are the key areas to focus on before placing your business on the market:

CURB APPEAL

The buyer will see the exterior of your business first. Take the time to ensure you are making a good first impression by improving your existing curb appeal. The following tips will help you maximize the profits you make on the sale of your business.

Parking Lots

Make sure the parking lot is clean. This is important, cost effective, and easy, and, boy, does it make a difference. When buyers drive up to your parking lot, it is one of the first things they see. If your parking lot is dirty and filled with trash, they have formed a negative opinion before even walking into the business. We once showed a physical therapy practice that was in a strip mall that also had a bar. We pulled up to meet the buyer and seller on a Saturday. Guess what we almost drove over? A man was drunk and passed out in the parking lot in front of the physical therapy practice. We immediately called 911, and then we called the buyer to reschedule the meeting due to an emergency. Can you imagine what the buyers would have thought if they had discovered the passed-out stranger?

Sidewalks

Make sure the sidewalk is clean. The sidewalk is the second thing buyers look at. Again, it sets the stage for what's inside. If the parking lot and curb look spick-and-span, the buyer will walk into the business with a positive attitude before even opening the door.

Front Door

Make sure the front door is clean. We know this all sounds like common sense; however, common sense is not as common as it once was. If the parking lot and curb are clean but the front door is filthy or has ugly decals, the buyer's perception has just changed from positive to negative that quickly, and they still haven't opened the door. Make sure the door and any glass in the door are very clean. Paint the door, if necessary. These are all inexpensive fixes that will earn you money at the closing table.

Windows

Make sure the windows are clean. The windows are as important as the front door. Many of us are window shoppers, and we like to take a sneak peek before we walk in. I'm not referring to just small businesses here; buyers will do a drive-by to inspect larger businesses after hours as well. If they don't like what they see, they will call to reschedule the meeting, but they are really canceling the meeting. Make sure your windows are clean and have minimal signage. Too much signage and stickers on windows and doors is a huge distraction and not necessary.

Advertising

We once worked with a large graphics and printing company that we were selling for millions. The problem was they were advertising everything they did on their windows, doors, and the side of the building. Their need to advertise everything on the outside was causing buyers to walk away from their business before seeing the inside. Remember: Less is more when trying to sell your company.

Visibility of Signage

Make sure the name of the company is visible. All businesses, regardless of size, need proper signage. Without proper signage, your buyers will not be able to find your location easily. Signage should be as big as your landlord and city ordinance will permit. If you are in an area with a lot of trees and shrubbery, hire a gardener to trim them back and clean it up. Buyers and customers need to see your sign, not your pretty landscaping. Although pretty landscaping does help curb appeal, it should not block your sign, door, sidewalk, or business.

If you are in a strip mall, you need to have a sign on the strip mall's pylon so your buyers and consumers can locate your business. Your signage should be clean and current, not antiquated. Another recommendation if your business is in a strip mall is to have a smaller sign on your door so your customers and buyers can find your business easier. Many times, it seems that the larger the business, the smaller the sign. We can't begin to tell you how many times we or our buyers have tried to find a potential seller's business and have had to call an owner due to poor or no signage.

PROPER STAGING INSIDE

Make sure the inside is clean. Once you have handled creating a positive impression from the outside, take time to set the stage for what's inside. You want the buyer to walk in and feel comfortable and to get the sense that you care about the environment of your business and the working environment for your employees. If the inside is dirty and cluttered, what will a potential buyer expect to find when they review your accounting records?

Floors

Make sure the floors are clean. Painted concrete, hardwood floors, and tile all look good when clean and are easy to clean and shine. Carpet is typically an issue. If the carpet is stained, hire a professional to clean it. When carpet is stained or ripped, it gives the appearance that the business is dirty. There may be a lot of traffic, but buyers will wonder why, if the owner is making money like they say they are, they haven't replaced the carpet. Buyers will form their own perceptions on a multitude of details they see in your business. The more positives we can show, the more cash they will show at the closing table.

Walls and Ceilings

It's amazing how dirty walls and doors become and what a bad impression it leaves on buyers. Hire a cleaning crew to spruce them up and make everything look new. Buyers will eyeball your entire space, including the ceiling. We have seen many businesses that look great until you look up and the ceiling tiles are missing. Go the extra mile and replace the ceiling tiles; again, it is a cheap fix that, in the end, will be worth it.

Inventory

Retail locations should be stocked with inventory. There is nothing worse than bringing a buyer to see a grocery, convenience, clothing, or jewelry store and the shelves, racks, or displays are empty. The buyers will automatically think that the seller has fallen on hard times and can't afford to stock the shelves. If your shelves are empty, the buyer's pocketbook will be empty, and they won't make you an offer. Stock your shelves.

Dust

Shelves and inventory should be clean and free of dust. Have your employees dust the shelves and inventory weekly. Our firm showed a multimillion-dollar, all-in-one property that included a grocery store, a deli, and a gas station to a potential buyer. The shelves and inventory were covered with dust. It appeared as if no one had been shopping there for years. This buyer was not impressed and fussed about all the dust. Our team told our seller that we could not and would not show the business again until they cleaned it up.

YOU TOO, BLUE-COLLAR INDUSTRIES

Many manufacturing, trucking, construction, fabrication, and other companies are not the most appealing businesses to show buyers. However, many of these businesses come with multimillion-dollar price tags. Most of these businesses have a small office with a warehouse or plant attached to it. Many have no air conditioning or heat. Some of these buildings are covered in sheet metal and are certainly not attractive.

Our sellers always tell us, "It is what it is; we can't do anything to spruce it up." We disagree. You might not be able to stage it and make it look pretty, because let's face it, it is a shop, but you can certainly clean it. Power wash the floors, and clean the bathrooms so they look presentable. Most importantly, clean the office. Create a nice space that the buyer can emotionally connect to—a place where they can see themselves running your company. These are all easy, cost-effective solutions that will improve the look and feel of your business and leave your buyers with a good perception and wanting to see more. So, take the time to properly prep your business for sale, and address each key area mentioned.

KNOW MORE TO EXIT RICH

Staging your business for sale is crucial if you want to earn top dollar on the sale of your company. Since selling your business is one of the most important financial decisions you will ever make, take the time and effort now to create a good first impression for prospective buyers so that when they visit your business, they will feel confident they are purchasing something of value and will make a fair offer.

DID YOU KNOW?

- According to a study performed by Princeton psychologists, first impressions form in less than a second.

- According to Growth Business, cleaning professionals say that getting rid of excess clutter would eliminate 40 percent of cleaning work needed.

- According to Motherly, clutter can also trigger the release of the stress hormone cortisol, which can increase tension and anxiety and lead to unhealthy habits.

IMPLEMENTATION IS KEY

To further explore the lessons learned in this chapter, implement the following:

- Have your advisor provide a punch list of what needs to be cleaned and fixed on both the outside and inside of your company.

- Engage your employees or contract with a company to make all changes on the punch list.

- Enlist your advisor to conduct a walkthrough of the business before showing to any prospective buyers.

To download your free copy of the "How to Stage Your Business" checklist, visit SeilerTuckerAcademy.com.

How to Package Your Business for Sale

"Packaging can be theater; it can create a story."
—**Steve Jobs**

Prospective buyers need marketing materials on your business—a detailed catalogue of your business's strengths and areas of opportunity. You need to identify and document everything possible about your business.

It's imperative to have good paper when you put your business on the market. Many business and real estate brokers often provide buyers with information that is scattered and piecemeal, when what is needed is a carefully crafted and detailed CIM.

Marketing materials are designed to provide information to whet the buyer's appetite and answer most buyers' questions. Because many individuals are visually minded, make sure you include color photos, graphs, and charts. Be sure to include photos of the inside and outside of the business, because this helps increase the likelihood of a sale.

Include descriptions of what you offer, and include any other brochures or marketing pieces that provide a picture of your products and services.

You create marketing materials as the first step in the selling of your business. Marketing materials are not designed to sell the business; they're created to leave buyers wanting more.

THE KEY ELEMENTS TO INCLUDE IN YOUR MARKETING PACKAGE

We will now learn about the key elements to include in your marketing package. You'll notice that many of the following are based on the ST 6 P's.

- Ownership: All owners, along with their percentage of ownership, must be listed in the CIM.

- Entity: You will want to state what type of business you are. For example, is your business an LLC, an S or C corporation, a partnership, or a sole proprietorship?

- Years in business (proprietary): Be sure to include when your business was established and how long you have owned it.

- Location (proprietary): When creating your marketing package, you'll want to include the location of your business and how long you have been in that location. You'll also want to include whether you own the real estate and whether it is for sale. If not, state if there is a lease, including the lease terms, how much the rent is, and whether there is an option to renew. Buyers will also want to know if the landlord will allow a transfer or agree to a sublease. And last, you'll want to include if the business can be relocated and what the relocation expenses would be.

- Business summary (proprietary): You will want to state what your business does and what makes your products and services unique.

- Industry facts (product): Describe your industry, including its strengths and weaknesses and whether your products or services and industry are on the way up or out.

- Exclusive rights and growth potential (intellectual property and profits): It's important to know your exclusive rights and growth potential. For example, what exclusive rights do you have secured by intellectual property protection that provide you a competitive advantage? What is the growth potential of your business and industry? What would it take to catapult your business to the next level?

- Competition (proprietary and patrons): It's important to know your competition. Find out who they are and what makes your products and services different from your competitors'. Ask what a buyer can do to grow more market share.

- Client base (patrons): To determine your client base, ask yourself these questions: Does your business follow the 80/20 rule? Who are your customers? How much of your business is repeat business? Do they do business with you because of brand loyalty, location loyalty, price, quality, customer service, or all of the above? How far do they travel to buy your products and services? Using charts and graphs, provide client demographics, including age, sex, income, and customer radius.

EXAMPLE CUSTOMER CONCENTRATION CHART

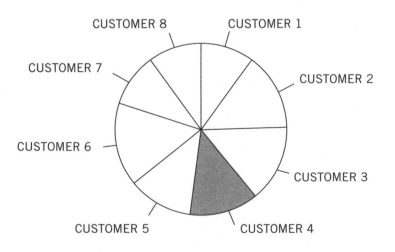

- Revenue (profits): Find out what percentage of your revenue comes from what percentage of your clients. To do this,

  ○ Pull customer reports from QuickBooks or your financial software, remove their names, and chart their monthly spending and the percentage of total sales they represent.

  ○ You want to show the prospective buyer that you do not derive or depend on most of your revenue from only one or two customers.

  ○ Provide a breakdown of your client base. You might have a chart showing the percentage of customers in different categories. For example, you could have 65 percent of your business in government contracts, 25 percent in commercial clients, and the rest in schools.

EXAMPLE REVENUE CONCENTRATION CHART (PER LOCATION)

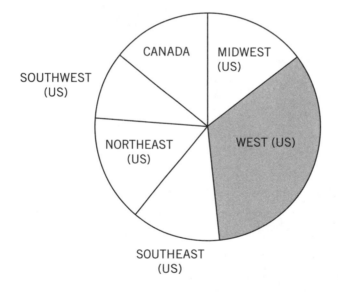

- New clients (patrons): You'll also want to include how you obtain new clients, how much it costs to acquire each new client, and what you do to get them.
- Contracts in place (proprietary): Be sure to include how many

contracts you have in place, as well as their lengths and terms and whether they are transferable or not.

- Product mix (products): Here, you will want to include whether you have multiple revenue streams. Use a graph to show the percentage of the business that comes from each profit center. For example, we sold an air conditioning and manufacturing company. Their business was 50 percent A/C and 50 percent manufacturing.

EXAMPLE PRODUCT MIX CHART

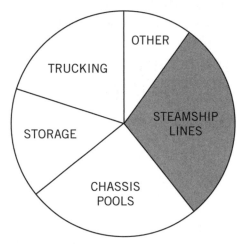

- Industry (product): If you're in a specialized industry, such as A/C and heating manufacturing, let prospective buyers know if the company can be split up and sold to different buyers. An HVAC technician might love to buy just the A/C and heating division, for example, whereas many manufacturing companies would be interested in the manufacturing business alone.

- Logos, trademarks, trade secrets, patents (proprietary): Identify your logo and trademarks. Make it clear whether you have trade secrets, but don't disclose them before you close on the business. A restaurant can say it has dozens of recipes, for example, but it shouldn't give them away until the deal is done. That way, if the buyer wants the secrets, they must first buy the business. If you have any patents or patents pending, be sure to list them.

- Databases (proprietary): Describe your proprietary database and the number of contacts, but do not disclose the individual names or other confidential information before the deal is finalized.

- Seasonality: Determine whether your business is seasonal. If so, which season, and how long does it last? Be sure to include the types of revenue you generate in the busy season as compared to the slow season. You'll also want to disclose how much working capital is needed during the slow season and whether you can introduce any other profit centers or congruent revenue streams in the slow season to generate more revenue.

- Advertising: In the marketing package, it is also important to state whether you advertise. You'll want to include the methods of advertising you use, as well as your advertising budget and whether you get co-op money for advertising, including the amount. If a buyer were to grow the business, they will want to know which advertising methods or vehicle to use, so be as specific as you can.

- Internet presence (proprietary): These days, a strong Internet presence is paramount. You'll want to make sure your website is current. Other things you can include are who does the web hosting, whether you sell products online, whether you engage in social media, and who manages your social media accounts. Buyers will want to know if they can grow your business online, so if you are already well positioned in this area, it will make your business that much more appealing to them.

- Employees and management team (people): Use an organizational chart to describe your management team and employees. List who your employees are, as well as their tenure, job title, and pay. The larger the company, the more detailed you need to be regarding your employees. You will need to disclose the following information in your marketing package:

  ○ The number of employee contracts

- ○ The number of noncompete agreements

- ○ The number of independent contractors and how they are paid

- ○ A detailed account of all employee benefits

- ○ A description of your employee retention rate

- ○ Whether you have a human resources manager on staff

- ○ How much it costs you to hire and train new staff

- ○ Larger companies also need to identify their key personnel, such as CEO, CFO, COO, chief of marketing, and chief of technology. Many companies use different or varied titles for the same positions. Be sure to identify and explain these.

INCLUDE A SWOT ANALYSIS IN YOUR CONFIDENTIAL INFORMATION MEMORANDUM

When preparing to sell your business, you will need to create a SWOT analysis to include in your CIM. SWOT stands for *strengths, weaknesses, opportunities,* and *threats*. A SWOT analysis is a strategic planning technique that can help you identify specific strengths and weaknesses, as well as opportunities and threats to your business. Undergoing this analysis will help you pinpoint any internal or external factors that could prevent you from achieving a successful exit. When undergoing your analysis, keep the following in mind: It's imperative to keep your clients in mind, because they are your best resource as it relates to their perceived strengths and weaknesses of your business. What you think are your strengths and weaknesses are your perceptions, but what your clients think is your true reality.

When you evaluate your opportunities, look at your competitors and what they are doing that you could implement to improve your business. Also evaluate your consumers' needs. For example, ask what your consumers are looking for, what problems they need you to solve, and what would make their lives easier. As far as threats go, look at technology and competition. Can your industry be replaced with technology, or can a competitor come in and scoop you up like Uber did to the taxi industry?

STRENGTHS

Use the ST 6 P's (people, product, process, proprietary, patrons, and profits) to identify your business strengths and what makes your business unique. Make your strengths stand out clearly.

WEAKNESSES

Rebrand any weaknesses as opportunities for growth by providing ideas on how they can grow the business and make it even better.

OPPORTUNITIES

Identify the potential in your business or industry and how to increase it.

THREATS

Clearly identify possible threats and how to overcome them. If you don't point them out in the beginning, buyers will find them during due diligence and think you are trying to hide facts. You must be transparent and disclose the good, the bad, and the ugly.

SWOT CHART

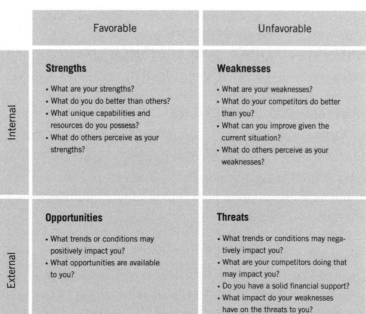

	Favorable	Unfavorable
Internal	**Strengths** • What are your strengths? • What do you do better than others? • What unique capabilities and resources do you possess? • What do others perceive as your strengths?	**Weaknesses** • What are your weaknesses? • What do your competitors do better than you? • What can you improve given the current situation? • What do others perceive as your weaknesses?
External	**Opportunities** • What trends or conditions may positively impact you? • What opportunities are available to you?	**Threats** • What trends or conditions may negatively impact you? • What are your competitors doing that may impact you? • Do you have a solid financial support? • What impact do your weaknesses have on the threats to you?

Some additional items to include in the buyer's marketing packet:

TRAINING AFTER THE SALE (PEOPLE)

Identify a training period for the new owner, explaining that its length depends on your industry, the special skills needed, and the buyer's experience and core competencies. Also, disclose your willingness to stay on as an employee or consultant.

FRANCHISE INFORMATION

If your business is a franchise, include pertinent information, such as franchise corporate headquarters, franchisee qualifications, application process, training, transfer fee, and closing protocol and cost.

NONCOMPETE CLAUSES

Buyers need assurances that you're not going to sell the business, cash out, and then compete against them. Get advice from an M&A advisor or business broker or attorney regarding what is enforceable in your state, and be prepared to outline the noncompete provisions that you'll agree to. Be careful that you do not negotiate against yourself by volunteering information about your willingness to agree to a noncompete provision too early in the negotiation process.

FURNITURE, FIXTURES, AND EQUIPMENT LIST

Include an up-to-date schedule of the FF&E that's included in the sale.

FINANCIALS AND PROJECTIONS

Show the buyer your true seller's discretionary income, adjusted EBITDA, or EBIT by including a three- to five-year financial snapshot based on your tax returns and P&L statements, including your add-backs. Make sure to include two- to three-year projections and a current balance sheet. Consult a professional when doing projections.

PRICE AND TERMS

The last page of your marketing materials should include a price and terms sheet outlining your expectations. Disclose the price and terms and what is included, such as the FF&E, inventory, real estate (if applicable), accounts receivable, and any other intellectual property. It should also state any transfer fees (if your business is a franchise). Also, indicate the seller financing terms you are willing to accept. And if you were able to get your business lender prequalified, be sure to include that as well.

MENTORING CORNER

Preparing a CIM may sound time consuming, but it will actually save you time and may help you identify areas that need attention before a potential sale. You may have several buyers interested in your business, so preparing duplicate sets of information for them will not only save you time but will help you make sure you are providing them all with the same information.

When mentoring clients, Sharon suggests that they provide information in two stages, with different levels of detail. This approach will help the broker, as well as potential buyers, and can prevent the inadvertent disclosure of confidential information.

The first level of information is compiled in what Sharon refers to as the Look Book and includes only marketing information about your business that is public knowledge but brought together in a concise presentation about your business, your reputation, and your market and industry. The Look Book can be provided to all interested prospective buyers.

The second level of information is compiled in what Sharon calls a Due Diligence Book and includes the information that Michelle lists in the SWOT analysis, along with any other information that a buyer would find pertinent to evaluating the business. The Due Diligence Book includes confidential information that a broker will need and that a buyer will want to review. However, it would be provided to a prospective buyer only after they have signed a confidentiality agreement—and preferably an LOI. The book is indexed, and each page is marked *CONFIDENTIAL*. This allows your team of attorneys and accountants a reference when dealing with and communicating with potential buyers as the deal moves forward.

Michelle has laid out a great outline for creating the marketing tools for your business in this chapter. Address each item in the SWOT analysis, and you will save a lot of back-and-forth communication with a potential buyer.

KNOW MORE TO EXIT RICH

In this chapter, we learned how to package your business for sale. Prospective buyers will want comprehensive marketing materials on your business to assess your business's strengths and opportunities. Therefore, you will need to identify and document everything possible about your business and showcase your findings in your Look Book. These materials are the first step in the selling of your business, and if done properly, they will leave your buyers wanting more.

DID YOU KNOW?

- According to Kinesisinc.com, a key part to making an effective prospectus is to identify the target market. To do this, you need a clear understanding of your company's core customer and how they can be found and marketed to. For example, ask yourself who your core customers are. What are their demographic or psychographic markers? Where do they congregate? What are their pain points? How does the business uniquely serve them? How is the company's current messaging strategy built to speak to their needs?

- Studies have shown that people can recall 65 percent of the visual content that they see almost three days later. In comparison, people can only recall about 10 percent of written content three days after it's read.

- Color increases brand recognition by up to 80 percent according to a study performed by the University of Loyola.

IMPLEMENTATION IS KEY

To further explore the lessons learned in this chapter, implement the following:

- Analyze your company using the SWOT analysis.
- Ensure that your company has a current organizational chart.
- Familiarize yourself with all the points of a CIM.
- Be sure to use lots of photos, graphs, charts, and color.

15

Confidentiality Is Key

"Confidentiality and transparency are not mutually exclusive but, rather, two sides of the same coin."

—Thomas de Maizière

Confidentiality is the number-one factor in protecting your business during the sales process. Once you've put all the work into figuring out what your business is worth and have created your CIM, don't make the mistake of disclosing information outside of a confidentiality agreement. Unfortunately, the biggest threat to your successful sale is the very thing that most people think is necessary for success: word of mouth. In other words, the more people you tell, the less likely you'll sell.

Word of mouth is important in sales, but it needs to be the right message at the right time. Otherwise, you lose control of how information is being spread, and the consequences can be disastrous. If you're selling your business by yourself, it's practically impossible to avoid breaching confidentiality, because you're not likely to qualify buyers or get them to sign binding nondisclosure agreements (NDAs). Without those safeguards, your prospective buyers will tell anyone and everyone that they're considering buying your business. What's so bad about that? The potential loss of any of the ST 6 P's! These P's are the value drivers. If any of them is weakened during the sales process, your price and position weaken too.

A breach of confidentiality can have a huge effect on a sale. A great benefit of hiring an M&A advisor or business broker is that it allows you to keep your employees insulated so they cannot negatively affect the sale.

DISCLOSURE IN THE CONTEXT OF THE ST 6 P'S: PEOPLE

As we learned earlier, people are one of the most crucial of the ST 6 P's. In this next section, we will explore this P by looking at its effect on employees, patrons, vendors, franchisors, landlords, professionals, and competitors.

EMPLOYEES

Consider the effect of the news of a sale on your employees, one of the crucial elements of the ST 6 P's. As we discussed earlier, if and when your employees hear from a third party that you're selling your business, they will get spooked. Imaginations will run wild. Employees will commiserate with each other and decide that the new owner may cut hours, fire them, or be difficult to work for. They can make the transition hard for the new owner or—worse—jump ship, leaving no one to run the company.

During one sale, we were representing an oil industry client and stressed that he not tell anyone—employees, customers, partners—that he was thinking of selling. But he always did the opposite of what we recommended, so he told *all* of them. One key employee quit right away. Another demanded a $40,000 raise and quit shortly after receiving it. This is exactly why we urge clients not to tell employees they're selling their business.

The owner's CFO needed to know they were selling, because she assisted with all the financial aspects of the sale. However, there was no reason to disclose the sale to the rest of the team. If any member of your management team needs to aid in the sale, such as preparing financials, have them first sign an NDA specifically relating to the sale.

PATRONS OR CUSTOMERS

Over time, your customers have grown used to your products, service, and quality. They like their relationship with you and your employees. And like employees, they don't like change. They are concerned that a new owner will alter things and no longer provide good service. The danger here is that if they start spreading their unfounded opinion, they can seriously damage your customer base and, with that, any future business a buyer is counting on. If the owners don't have a one-on-one relationship with their customers, this may not be as much of a problem as when the owner is thoroughly involved in day-to-day operations and in direct contact with them.

Don't tell customers your plans. Instead, the seller and buyer should tell customers that they've created a partnership (this is especially useful if you are owner financing the sale). Many times, the seller and buyer don't tell customers that the business has changed hands until several months or even several years later, when it doesn't matter.

VENDORS

Vendors can grow concerned when they hear your business is for sale. They may worry that the new owners will use their own vendors. Vendors are often uncertain about the new owner's ability to pay on time and are, therefore, leery about providing similar terms to the new owner. In many cases, vendors need to prequalify the buyer for the purchase of their products and services, which can affect the business going forward. This is especially true with distributors, who can decide whether they're comfortable with the buyer's financials, skill sets, and industry experience.

There's a catch-22 here. How do you get your vendors to prequalify a buyer without alerting them that the business is for sale? An M&A advisor or business broker, acting as a third party, can make this happen without revealing the business in question.

FRANCHISORS

News that a franchisee is selling worries the franchisor, because they are then responsible for teaching the new owner the franchise formula (e.g., how to run the business, what type of marketing is used, and the type of paperwork needed). Many franchise documents require franchisor approval before a franchisee can sell to a third party. The franchisor will also have to prequalify the buyer's financials, skill sets, and industry experience. And if the new owner isn't as good as the previous one, the franchisor could end up with lower royalties.

LANDLORDS

Landlords get spooked when a good tenant decides to sell their company. They are concerned that the new owner may not be as reliable when it comes to paying rent on time or taking care of their property. If your business is dependent on the location that you lease, your landlord needs to cooperate with your buyer. Not all landlords will, especially if they have the option to increase rental rates and terms. However, it is prudent to talk with your landlord and ensure they are agreeable to honoring a sublease or transfer or drafting a new lease. It's important to know in advance what their expectations are so you will be able to properly inform the buyer of the landlord's intention.

Keep in mind that, prior to the sale, the landlord will have to qualify your buyer's financials, credit history, skill sets, and industry experience before they agree to negotiate or finalize a new agreement. However, until you have a purchase offer or LOI with escrow money from the buyer, there is no reason to introduce the landlord and buyer to each other.

PROFESSIONALS

The attorneys and CPAs that you've worked with during the course of the year get nervous when they prematurely hear you're selling, because they become convinced the new owner will use their own team of professionals. This can create a potential conflict of interest.

Other times, sellers do not want to tell their CPA they are selling. However, in most cases, you will need to inform your accounting firm of your decision to sell, because you will need their assistance in gathering the financials and answering complex financial questions. If you don't engage their assistance in the beginning, you will certainly need their involvement during the due diligence period, because you'll need to prepare an audit of your books and records for the buyer (if the buyer doesn't hire a third-party forensic accountant). As a professional, your accountant and attorney will follow the code of ethics, which includes confidentiality.

COMPETITORS

The competition is a particularly significant reason to keep quiet, because they'll use leaked information against you. Unlike everyone else, competitors are ecstatic that you're selling. They might even tell their employees, vendors, and customers that you're going out of business and let the resulting confusion drive your business down while theirs goes up.

DISCLOSING CONFIDENTIAL INFORMATION

It's almost impossible for you to market your business for sale yourself without disclosing confidential information. One of the advantages of using an M&A advisor or business broker is that it is less likely that the fact that your business is for sale will become known. Few sellers have the discipline necessary to keep the possibility of a sale secret. When confidential information is disclosed, it is usually done by the seller, who tells someone, who, in turn, tells someone else. An M&A advisor or business broker rarely breaches confidentiality and can help steer you away from spilling too much or speaking to the wrong person.

Most sellers do not qualify buyers, nor do they get them to sign the proper nondisclosure documents. Therefore, these buyers will tell their friends, family, and everyone they meet that they're considering buying that business. And everyone ends up knowing prior to the sale, including the employees and competitors of the business.

For example, when we listed a medical practice for sale a few years ago, the owner was paranoid that his doctors would find out that his business was for sale. Of course, most (but not all) M&A advisors or business brokers take measures to ensure confidentiality. Two months after signing an engagement agreement with us, the owner called Michelle in the middle of the night in a panic. He asked, frantically, "Who else did you show the business to?"

"I've only shown your business to one prospect," she said.

"Then why do all of my doctors know that I'm thinking of selling my business?" He was beside himself.

Michelle then asked him, "Who did you tell?"

"I didn't tell anyone, other than my wife," he said.

Michelle suggested that he take a deep breath, get a good night's sleep, and think about anyone else he'd discussed selling his business with. He called her the next morning. "I told a close friend," he admitted sheepishly. "He's a doctor who sends me business."

Guess what? That doctor told another doctor, who told another doctor, who told another one, and so on. Before he knew it, news of the sale had spread like wildfire.

Remember: When selling your business, confidentiality can be essential to the success of the sale.

THE DOS AND DON'TS OF GETTING THE WORD OUT

Here's a paradox you must solve if you want to sell your business on your own: You can't sell your business if you keep the sale a secret, but if you tell anyone, you may end up with a business that can't be sold.

While you try to wrap your head around that, here are some tips to help you market your business as discreetly as possible and eliminate the most common mistakes sellers make:

DO NOT HIRE A REAL ESTATE AGENT

The real estate motto is "The more people I tell, the more I sell." Real estate agents typically place the business owner's ad on a real estate multiple listing service (MLS), rather than a business MLS. The real estate MLS is typically used for real estate, not businesses that are trying to maintain confidentiality, and is neither the most productive site to market businesses nor the most confidential, because, at a minimum, it includes the business's address. In addition, a real estate agent will put a sign in the front yard or window (if permitted) and will occasionally run an ad in the paper.

ADVERTISE DISCREETLY ON BUSINESS SITES

There are between ten and twenty business-related MLS sites. Do not advertise on a real estate MLS, because they require you to display the address of the location, thereby exposing your business and destroying any hope of maintaining confidentiality. Business MLSes, however, are different from real estate sites, because they do not require proprietary information to list your business. Place your business on all of them, if possible, to maximize visibility and attract as many buyers as you can. You will have to post your listing to each of these sites separately and pay a monthly fee for each site. You will also want to update your listings on a regular basis so they appear at the top of the list. However, most M&A advisors and business brokers will pay for the MLS fees and post and update your listing to all these different sites regularly, which will save you a tremendous amount of time, money, energy, and effort.

QUALIFY BUYERS

If you are attempting to sell your business on your own, you will have to screen all buyers from these sites to determine which are a good fit for your business. Again, this takes an enormous amount of time and energy, and it can lead to inadvertent disclosure of confidential information. Many potential buyers are tire kickers who are not qualified to buy your business. In addition, 95 percent of buyers do not buy the business that instigated their call. You will kiss a lot of frogs before you find a prince of a buyer to purchase your business. M&A advisors and business brokers, on the other hand, will have a lot more buyers, because they have a lot more inventory than that one business, which increases the odds of finding your prince.

ADVERTISE IN ONLINE NEWSPAPERS
AND TRADE JOURNALS

You can discreetly advertise in newspapers and trade journals (i.e., not divulging any proprietary information). You'll just need to determine what contact information you are going to include in the ad. Keep in mind that advertising is expensive, and you must advertise consistently to attract the right buyer.

HIRE A PROFESSIONAL, EXPERIENCED
M&A ADVISOR OR BUSINESS BROKER

The number-one reason sellers hire experienced M&A advisors and business brokers? We are successful at marketing businesses without breaching confidentiality.

FOR SALE BY OWNER: YES OR NO?

There are many factors to consider when selling your business. When deciding whether to go it alone, consider the following:

- What description can you use on the web without disclosing the fact that your business is for sale or other confidential information?
- What email address or phone number are you going to use in the ads?
- What fax number are you going to provide to potential prospects?
- What NDAs are you going to use?
- Where are you going to meet prospects?
- How are you going to confirm your contact?

It may be difficult to determine who is on the other end of the phone or an email address when communicating with a potential buyer. It could be an acquaintance, vendor, customer, or employee contacting you. Or it could be a competitor looking to buy a business or to obtain information about their competition. These individuals also look at businesses to purchase, but if they see a competitor's ad, they might act like an interested buyer to obtain information to create a competitive advantage instead.

Experienced M&A advisors and business brokers use their own database of qualified buyers and advertise your business confidentially. They only disclose your business to buyers who have signed confidentiality agreements and, most important, who have also qualified financially.

In some cases, it is best not to disclose any proprietary details regarding the business until the seller is comfortable with the buyer's financials, skill sets, and industry experience. An experienced broker facilitates this process by using blind CIMs and discreet conference calls with the buyer and seller before disclosing any proprietary information. In fact, we have gone as far as negotiating LOIs on a business that was sight unseen by the buyer.

Also, we don't show our client's business to any of their competitors without our seller's written permission to do so. We once sold an industrial staffing company that had offices throughout the United States. During the marketing process, we had hundreds of buyers, many our client's direct competitors. Some were sincerely interested, but others were just seeking details about their competition and their reasons for selling. Our seller would approve some buyers and disapprove others. We ended up selling their business to one of their larger competitors.

Some competitors will pose as buyers, but they are really interested in discovering everything they can about a business to compete with it. In some situations, you will need to have prospects sign not only an NDA but also a noncompete agreement.

You walk a fine line in determining how much information you should share with a buyer during different phases of the buying process. We have heard horror stories about sellers giving potential buyers all kinds of proprietary information regarding their industry, systems, procedures, vendors, and customer lists. At the end of the day, the buyers had everything they needed to compete against the seller.

Our firm implements a strategic and comprehensive marketing plan (undisclosed) for each of our individual businesses. We have a database of thousands of buyers for the seven different types of businesses. In addition, we have a database of private equity firms and strategic buyers. We also subscribe to a multitude of lists to implement strategic marketing campaigns, all while maintaining confidentiality for our clients.

MENTORING CORNER

We stress the importance of confidentiality throughout this book, because it is extremely important, as in the example in which a client told one doctor friend who, maliciously or not, caused the word to spread prematurely.

We want to emphasize the importance of what and how you tell your family as well, because of the added emotional elements that can play out. A conversation over dinner can be shared by your children with their friends at school or by a spouse talking to a friend they deem trustworthy. Sharon had a client who was preparing to sell his business, and his daughter innocently told her friends at school. One of those friends was the daughter of his largest customer, so imagine his surprise when he received a call from a very concerned customer the next day, causing unnecessary drama and headaches.

Confidentiality allows you to control the process of who knows and when they know what you are doing. The reason you want to establish a contractual obligation of confidentiality is that in the absence of an obligation of confidentiality, which typically must be created by a (written) agreement, there is no obligation to keep information secret. In fact, as a technical matter, you lose confidential status for any information divulged to someone who is not obligated to keep it confidential.

Sometimes it's difficult to get a prospective buyer to sign a confidentiality agreement. That's why it's good to have a Look Book, which does not contain confidential information. Once the buyer is truly interested in a good faith purchase, they will typically agree to a reasonable confidentiality agreement, particularly since the absence of the confidentiality agreement would affect their rights to the confidential information after the acquisition.

 **KNOW MORE TO EXIT RICH**

In this chapter, we covered the importance of maintaining confidentiality about the sale of your business to protect your greatest asset during the sales process. As you learned, the biggest threat to selling your business is word of mouth. After you've put all the hard work into figuring out what your business is worth and have prepared for the sale, don't make the mistake of telling others outside of a confidentiality agreement, because this could be detrimental to your business and cause your sale to unravel.

DID YOU KNOW?

- More than 66 percent of data leaks logged by InfoWatch Group in 2016 were brought about internally.

- According to LawTrades, many of the laws across the country that protect trade secrets and confidential commercial information are based on the Uniform Trade Secrets Act.

- According to MidStreet Mergers and Acquisitions, you should wait to tell your employees that you're selling your business until after you have officially sold it, to avoid them looking for other work.

IMPLEMENTATION IS KEY

To further explore the lessons learned in this chapter, implement the following:

- Don't tell anyone you're selling your business, other than your professional team.

- If you are selling on your own, have your attorney draft an NDA and a noncompete agreement.

- Make sure you financially qualify all buyers.

- Don't market your business for sale without taking all the necessary precautions mentioned in this chapter.

GOLDEN NUGGET

—————————————⓰————————————

Qualifying and Educating Buyers

*"Education is the most powerful weapon
which you can use to change the world."*
—Nelson Mandela

A qualified, educated buyer is your best buyer. The more they know and the more they're invested, the less likely they will be to back out of the deal due to cold feet. Experienced M&A advisors and business brokers first qualify then educate prospective buyers to ensure that they are ready, able, and willing to buy and, most importantly, that they can close on the sale of the business.

LEVELS OF BUYER QUALIFICATION

As mentioned before, it's imperative to know who your buyer is, along with their buying criteria. Different types of buyers will require different levels of qualification and education.

FIRST-TIME BUYERS

We spend a lot of time qualifying first-time buyers. Most of them are skittish and require much hand-holding before they pull the trigger. In addition, many first-time buyers are not qualified to purchase a business. In these instances, pursuing a sale with them would simply be a waste of time for all involved.

Most first-time buyers have no idea how much they can afford to put down on a business. Therefore, a good M&A advisor or broker will walk them through the following qualification steps to see if they are in a good position to purchase a business.

FINANCIAL QUALIFICATION

Most of our businesses are lender prequalified or seller financed; therefore, we know the required down payment and collateral. We walk first-time buyers through filling out our financial statement, and we determine how much they can put down and finance based on their credit score, assets, and liabilities.

There are creative ways to finance deals. We work with buyers to obtain home equity loans and borrow against their retirement funds (without paying interest and penalties), and we introduce them to a variety of lenders that can help finance the deal. Keep in mind that just because the buyer may have a million to invest does not mean they will part with their million. It's crucial to determine how much they are comfortable putting down. That's why it's imperative to determine their WHY.

If a buyer tells you they can get the money from a third party, such as a family member, partner, or investor, insist that the investor come to the table with financial statements, sign an NDA, and convince you of their willingness to make this investment. If they don't, walk away.

THE WHY QUALIFICATION

As we mentioned above, you must determine the motivating factor—why they want to own a business. If their WHY is not powerful enough, they will never part with their hard-earned money. Their WHY must be so strong that it drowns out the naysayers, along with the negative voices in their head. Most first-time buyers are not confident enough to take that next step into entrepreneurship. Therefore, they ask their friends and family what they should do, and in most cases, their circle of influence (people who have no business experience) will advise them that they're making a horrible decision and that they should keep their day job and work toward retirement instead.

For example, we had a prospective buyer call us to buy a restaurant. We financially qualified her then asked her why she wanted to own a business. We also verified that she and her team had the core competencies needed to be successful. She had worked in banking for thirty-plus years and was close to retirement. Her friends and family kept telling her that she should never buy a business; she could lose her life's savings. They told her to stay at her corporate job for two more years until retirement. Michelle asked her why she wanted to buy a business when she was so close to retirement.

Here's what she said: "I've been in the same industry for over thirty years, making a little over a hundred thousand a year. My husband was exposed to Agent Orange and, according to his doctors, has outlived their prognosis. Once he passes, I will lose his benefits and income. Based on my retirement package, I can't afford my lifestyle." She went on to say, "I have worked over thirty years with nothing to show for it. I want to buy a business and grow a legacy for my daughter and her family."

Is that a powerful WHY? And is it powerful enough to keep her motivated so she can overcome naysayers and other landmines? It absolutely is! This buyer had no experience in running restaurants. She was attracted to the food industry because she thought it was easy. Anyone who knows restaurants knows it's anything but. Her core competencies were in management, sales, marketing, and finance. She wanted to buy a company within ninety days. She managed to save $350,000 to invest in a business. She was comfortable investing $300,000 and keeping $50,000 for working capital. She wanted to make more than her current salary of $100,000 yearly. Now that we knew her financial capacity (her WHY, her core competencies, and her time frame), we were able to find the right business (not a restaurant) that met all her buying criteria.

We helped her buy a flooring company with real estate that operated on all the ST 6 P's. The sellers accepted $300,000 down, and the seller financed the balance at 7 percent interest. The owners didn't have any debt, so they took less down and agreed to finance the balance. Their note was secure and in first position on their FF&E and property.

It all worked out beautifully: Her desired down payment was accepted. The business cash flowed enough to support the debt service. After debt service, the business cash flowed over $250,000 to support her lifestyle. She received her initial ROI in under two years, and she was able to grow the business and is now earning even more.

Keep in mind that it's not about the industry; it's about aligning the buyer's criteria with a business that matches it. A restaurant would not have been in her best interest, nor would it have matched her Buyer's Sanity Check, so we advised her to purchase the flooring company, and it worked out well for both her and the seller.

CORE COMPETENCY QUALIFICATION

You must qualify buyers on their strengths and weaknesses. As we mentioned in the story above, the buyer did not have any flooring experience, but she did have many other core competencies that suited her for working on the business, not in it. If the business operates on the ST 6 P's, the new owner can focus on working to grow the company.

TIMING QUALIFICATION

Timing is everything for sellers. They've spent time using the ST 6 P's to tune up their business so it will earn maximum profit in minimum time. It's also imperative to know the buyer's timing for the purchase. We once had a first-time buyer call us, wanting to purchase one of our companies. We met with him and started the qualification process. We asked him about his time frame. He said he was retiring in a year and would not buy a business prior to that time. We told him that most of our offerings had employees and management teams and that he could purchase the business and oversee it while keeping his job. He was a type A personality and wanted to control everything; therefore, he was adamant about waiting a full year before purchasing a business. We informed him that he was premature in his search, because most of the businesses we could show him today wouldn't be around in a year. A year later, he came back to us and purchased a business. Timing is everything, and if the buyer is not ready, they will never pull the trigger.

LOCATION QUALIFICATION

First-time buyers are typically more focused on location than the other four types of buyers. Most first-time buyers prefer to buy a business in their area, so location is their biggest motivating factor.

PULLING-THE-TRIGGER QUALIFICATION

Once a business meets a buyer's criteria and the Buyer's Sanity Check, it's imperative that you make sure they will indeed pull the trigger and purchase your business. Many first-time buyers get cold feet and never purchase a company. That's why it's so important to know their WHY.

PREPARING BUYERS FOR DECISION MAKING

At some point in the buying process, someone must decide. It's important to know who on the buyer's team has the power to say yes, as well as who can put the kibosh on the deal. We tell buyers that the people involved in saying yes—spouses, partners, and investors—all need to participate in every part of the process, including getting financially qualified. There is no point in spending energy to get half of a team to say yes, only to start from nothing with the other half, who might still say no.

Qualifying the other four types of buyers is not as daunting. However, you must still qualify their financial capability, their WHY, and their timing. The other types of buyers could have timing constraints, because many of them are running their companies and evaluating and buying other businesses at the same time.

We were working with a strategic buyer who wanted to purchase our multimillion-dollar environmental company to roll up into their current portfolio and go public. They qualified on all levels except for timing. They were unable to buy the business for at least eight months. Our seller refused to wait that long, so we sold his company to another buyer.

EDUCATING BUYERS

After qualifying the buyers, it's now time to educate them. As a seller, you will need to inform the buyer about your industry, along with all the intricate details of running your company. Failure to thoroughly inform a prospective buyer about what is involved in running your business can lead to cold feet and the whole deal falling apart. You'll have wasted your time, energy, and effort and must start again. And, in most cases, business owners do not have backup buyers. In addition to educating buyers on your industry and the details of running your company, you will need to educate them on other areas, which we will cover in this section.

EXPLAIN THE SKILLS THAT BUYERS NEED

From the outside, it might look like running your business is somewhat straightforward and easy. However, depending on your industry, there are likely to be many specific skills, talents, and abilities required to make it all work, not to mention licenses and certifications. Therefore, it's important to take time to point out to buyers what they need to know and how well they need to know it to be successful in running your business without you.

TEACH THEM ABOUT CONFIDENTIALITY

As we covered in the last chapter, breaches of confidentiality can stop a sale dead in its tracks. To avoid this, our firm plays good cop–bad cop with buyers about confidentiality. The good cop nicely explains that breaching confidentiality is bad, because it will ruin the business they're buying before they've even bought it. The bad cop puts the fear of God into them, telling them that if they breach confidentiality, the seller could file a lawsuit against them, and we might have no choice but to join them. This has proven effective in preventing breaches of confidentiality.

TEACH THEM HOW TO CONDUCT TOURS OF THE BUSINESS

As you know from golden nugget 15 about confidentiality, there are good reasons that your employees should not know that you're selling the place where they work. For that reason, we explain to buyers that we'll only show them the company after office hours so no employees are aware of what's going on. If the seller is onboard with showing the business during business hours, we educate the buyer that we will go in under the pretense of a lender, investor, or insurance agent.

On the other hand, if the business is a retail operation, we suggest that buyers come in during business hours to buy products and services as though they were a customer, to get the best idea of how the business operates. Again, for reasons of confidentiality, we insist that they don't talk to any employees or carry any marketing materials, like the CIM, into the business.

TEACH THEM WHEN TO CONDUCT DUE DILIGENCE

A buyer conducts due diligence to valuate what's being sold and to protect their interest. We tell our qualified buyers that we'll allow them to do the majority of their due diligence, such as reviewing the CIM and financials, seeing the business, and getting the majority of their questions answered, up front. That way, they can make an offer feeling comfortable that their decision is based on education, research, and knowledge.

However, until they make that offer and submit their purchase offer or LOI with escrow money on the table, there's too much at stake. We won't allow the following forms of due diligence:

- Conducting an audit of the company's books and records
- Having discussions with customers, employees, or vendors
- Validating inventory
- Inspecting FF&E
- Obtaining real estate appraisals

- Conducting real estate inspections

- Conducting environmental inspections

- Meeting with the landlord to negotiate a lease

- Obtaining a commercial or Small Business Association (SBA) loan

- Obtaining franchise approval

TEACH BUYERS THE BUSINESS

Buyers need to know that there are regulatory, legal, or administrative complications and restrictions in particular industries. Therefore, it's important to let buyers know about these potential roadblocks and how to navigate them.

TEACH FIRST-TIME BUYERS ABOUT BUSINESS VALUATIONS, AND SHOW THE OTHER FOUR TYPES OF BUYERS HOW TO SUBSTANTIATE THE SELLER'S PRICE

We show buyers how we arrived at the asking price for the business, which includes the different formulas described in golden nugget 12, along with industry standards and business comps. The more buyers know and understand, the more comfortable they are paying what you're asking.

EDUCATE BUYERS ON THE VALUE DRIVERS

You will also need to educate buyers on the value drivers in your business. The more they know, the more they will pay. These drivers are as follows:

People

The more talented or tenured employees and management team a company has, the more it will drive up the multiple.

Products and Services

Industries on the way up drive value.

Years in Business

Depending on how long it's been in business, the price of a company increases by certain multiples.

Intellectual Property

It's important to know how much intellectual property, such as patents, logos, trademarks, contracts, and databases, is included in the sale.

Location, Location, Location

Businesses sell for more if they have a dynamite location secured with real estate or a solid lease in place.

Furniture, Fixtures, and Equipment

While FF&E depreciates significantly and is not usually worth what you think it is, it does have value, which could increase the multiple, thereby increasing the sales price.

Inventory

Inventory is included in the sale of the business, at cost, and will be adjusted upward or downward at closing, depending on the inventory count.

Accounts Receivables

Money that is owed to the business could be considered an asset, but only if the seller can demonstrate a healthy collection rate on an aging report of one to three years' history; otherwise, the buyer could become a collection agency to get that accounts receivable value that was paid for. Also, accounts receivable might not be included if the buyer is negotiating to pay less than the asking price.

Accounts Payable

Accounts payable associated with accounts receivable is paid by the buyer. Accounts payable associated with collected accounts receivable is paid by the seller, as are company debt and lines of credit. In a stock sale, all equipment leases are assumed by the buyer. Again, as stated in previous chapters, this can be a point of contention, depending on the buyer.

Working Capital

It's also important to educate buyers on the different formulas to determine how much working capital is needed in the business and when. This is important because the buyer might not have enough working capital to operate the business, which could cause the business to fail. In addition, a buyer could have an unrealistic expectation on working capital, which could decrease the sales price of the business, causing the sale to be no longer viable for the seller. If we don't get working capital from the beginning (at the LOI phase), in all likelihood, the deal will fall apart during due diligence, because they won't be able to agree on working capital.

Franchise Transfer Timing and Fees

If you're buying a franchise, your offer should be contingent on franchise approval, because you typically can't close on a franchise until you've been approved as a franchisee, have signed the franchise disclosure document, and have completed your training. This can take three to six months. You also need to negotiate who will pay the transfer fee. Typically, it's the buyer.

EDUCATE FIRST-TIME BUYERS ON FINANCING OPTIONS AND REQUIREMENTS

Most of the other four types of buyers will have their financing already lined up when they are ready to purchase a business. First-time buyers can acquire financing, but who they get to fund the transaction will depend on certain factors. Preferred lenders with lower interest rates don't lend unless the perfect storm has occurred.

THE PERFECT STORM

The financial world can be a difficult one to navigate when you are looking to obtain financing to purchase a business. Lenders' main concerns are protecting their money and ensuring the debt gets paid back. Back in 2008, during the recession and the financial crisis, banks pretty much stopped lending unless the perfect storm occurred, which was when the seller had perfect books and records and the buyer had perfect credit and industry experience and could put down 100 percent. For the perfect storm to occur, all the stars have to align. It's been over ten years since the financial crisis, and banks will be much more lenient until the next crisis happens. The following shows how all the criteria for both the buy side and sell side line up for the perfect storm.

THE SELL SIDE

On the sell side, the following criteria must be met in order to obtain financing:

- The seller has the required net income with few add-backs.
- The business's cash flow must support the debt service and cover the buyer's living expenses.
- The industry is growing, not dying.
- The business has longevity.
- The seller can pay off all existing debt out of the closing proceeds.

THE BUY SIDE

On the buy side, for financing to be obtained, the following must occur:

- The buyer must have great credit history.
- The buyer must have cash on hand for a 10 to 20 percent down payment.
- The buyer must have enough collateral to secure the loan.
- Lenders also prefer that buyers have experience in the industry they are pursuing.

FINANCING OPTIONS

There are several financing options available to buyers when looking to purchase a business. Some of them include the following:

SMALL BUSINESS ADMINISTRATION LENDING

The SBA is a great resource with preferred lenders nationwide. They are great for first-time buyers, because they require 10 to 20 percent down. However, they may require the seller to hold an additional 10 percent subordinated to the SBA. Keep in mind that the seller will have a second position on their assets; SBA will be in first. If the seller owns real estate and the buyer defaults on their loan, the bank has the first position on getting paid. The seller is behind the lender on collecting in case of default; SBA's interest is typically 2 percent above prime and is variable. The buyer will have to secure the loan with their personal or business assets. The downside to this type of loan is that the SBA loan can take as long as six months to close and is paperwork intensive. For example, the preferred lender will require the seller's financials, their CIM, and the buyer's resume and business plan.

COMMERCIAL LENDERS

Most commercial lenders prefer not to deal with first-time buyers, because the other four types of buyers are more experienced and have capital and collateral to secure the loan. However, there are different lenders that will work with first-time buyers and risky industries, but their interest rates are higher than SBA and commercial lenders. All commercial lenders will require the seller to hold a second position on their assets while they are in first position in case of default.

BORROWING AGAINST A RETIREMENT FUND

First-time buyers can buy a business or obtain their down payment of 40 to 60 percent of the purchase price by borrowing from their retirement fund. The best part about this is that they won't have to pay taxes or penalties to do so.

HOME EQUITY LOAN

First-time buyers can use the equity in their home to buy the business or to obtain the down payment needed to purchase the business. Because it's a bank loan, the lender will take several things into consideration—most importantly, the buyer's ability to repay the loan from their current income and whether they're keeping their job. The reason for the loan is also a factor in getting it approved, so the bank is likely to ask for the business's financials. The amount of the loan also depends on an appraisal of the house that's securing it and whether it's possible that its sale could satisfy the outstanding mortgage and the amount of the loan.

SELLER FINANCING

One of the most competitive forms of financing is seller financing. Seller financing is the quickest, easiest way to sell a business. Most buyers are educated on this option, and it is their preference. However, many advisors and brokers do not protect the interest of the seller, because they just want to get the sale done. Our firm goes the extra mile in ensuring our seller's interest is protected. We educate the buyer on the collateral they will have to pledge to secure financing. The other good thing about the seller becoming the bank through seller financing is that the seller will be in first position.

EDUCATING BUYERS ON MAKING AN OFFER

It's important that buyers are informed about their purchase before making an offer. An uneducated buyer is a buyer who will never buy. In addition to the money, there are other factors to consider when making an offer, including the seller's state of mind and point of view and whether it is an asset sale or a stock sale.

THE SELLER'S STATE OF MIND AND POINT OF VIEW

As we mentioned in golden nugget 2, buyers need to understand that a seller wants to make sure they're leaving their baby in good hands and that the new owner will take care of their employees and clients. Buyers also need to understand that the seller needs to be compensated fairly for operating on all the ST 6 P's. Their brand, years in business, location, proprietary systems, patents, trademarks, proven systems, customer base, employees in place, and the time, energy, and effort they have put into the business should all be considered when making an offer.

When a buyer negotiates heavily on the asking price and then asks the seller to share the risk by providing seller financing, it makes the likelihood of a sale much more difficult. We always tell our buyers that you can't have your cake and eat it too. We once had a buyer that kept trying to negotiate over $200,000 of the purchase price and wanted the seller to carry 60 percent seller financing. Luckily, we had a backup buyer; the seller did have to provide financing, but he got much closer to his asking price.

ASSET SALE OR STOCK SALE?

As we mentioned previously, an asset sale concerns the purchase of the assets of a business, whereas a stock sale concerns ownership interest in the business itself.

Buyers prefer asset sales, because they don't want to be liable for any lawsuits, liabilities, or outstanding taxes that happened on the seller's watch, and they can depreciate the assets. To make this happen, the buyer forms a new business entity doing business as the existing company's name.

Sellers, however, prefer stock sales, because it decreases their tax liability. Keep in mind that stock sales become necessary if the business has contracts, licenses, workers' comp insurance in the company name, and an employer identification number that can't be transferred to another entity.

COMPONENTS NEEDED DURING AN OFFER

It's important to educate the buyer on the following so that they know what components are needed during the offer:

Escrow

Buyers must put up escrow money, usually 10 percent of the agreed purchase price in smaller transactions. Escrow is always contingent on due diligence. Many buyers of larger companies will not put down 10 percent, because they are putting in many offers at once.

Contingencies

An offer should contain various contingencies that would enable the buyer to withdraw from a deal without penalty if certain conditions of the sale are not met. Possible contingencies include obtaining a new lease, getting franchise approval, auditing the financials, and financing. In the event any of the buyer's contingencies are not met, the buyers are entitled to get their escrow deposit back in two to three business days, and there is no deal.

EDUCATING BUYERS ABOUT THE CLOSING PROCESS

Closing is a crucial part of the sale of your business. It is important that buyers are educated on getting to the finish line: closing. The sections below will help you walk your buyers through this process.

COMPLETING DUE DILIGENCE

Before closing, there is a due diligence period, typically thirty to ninety days with an agreed-upon expiration date, during which the buyer investigates and satisfies the contingencies in the agreement. After the due diligence period ends, the buyer is obligated to continue the purchase agreement or to forfeit escrow. It's imperative to hire an expert to facilitate due diligence. In medium to larger deals, the due diligence process can become quite complicated and drawn out.

CLOSING ATTORNEY AND CLOSING DOCUMENTS

Both parties should have their own attorneys support them during the due diligence phase and then review the closing documents, which includes the purchase agreement and all other related documents needed to close. It is important that the attorneys not try to renegotiate the deal at this point, because the price and terms have already been agreed upon.

We prefer that the only attorney involved in the actual closing be the one who represents the transaction, not the buyer or seller, and that this attorney do so for a flat fee. It is this attorney's job to make sure there are no outstanding liabilities or tax issues and to construct the legal closing documents, based on the purchase offer agreement (POA) or letter of intent (LOI).

This is where things tend to get tricky. If the buyer and seller both hire their own attorney, the two attorneys usually end up trying to renegotiate the deal and raise obstacles and create issues that didn't exist. Most attorneys bill per hour; the more issues they cause, the more they increase their bill.

We represented a multimillion-dollar medical company, and our firm recommended an attorney that was going to facilitate the close and not represent either party. The attorney would represent the transaction and charge a flat fee of $5,000 for the closing. The buyer was insistent on using a family friend. We inquired whether the buyer's attorney had any experience in representing and preparing closing documents for business closings. He informed us that the attorney did not have that type of experience; however, he worked for a large corporate firm.

The seller ended up hiring his own attorney. In turn, the buyer's attorney caused the closing to be delayed by two weeks. He constantly tried to renegotiate the deal. He was extremely unprofessional; he yelled and cursed at everyone. In fact, the attorney went so far as to say he did not want to do the deal. Of course, that is where we had to step in and tell the attorney to back off, because this was not his deal to do.

We then pulled both the buyer and the seller into a separate room and proceeded to ask them whether they wanted to continue with the transaction. They both said yes, but they were extremely frustrated that the attorney was renegotiating everything that they had already agreed to. Our firm told the buyer that he needed to control his attorney. The attorney worked for him, not the other way around. We then said that if we continued down this path, nothing would get resolved, and the buyer and seller would end up having animosity toward each other.

The buyer decided to control his attorney. Needless to say, the deal got done, but not without an expensive price tag. Remember: We had an attorney that agreed to a flat fee of $5,000 to facilitate the entire transaction. The buyer's attorney, however, charged him a whopping $35,000, and the seller's attorney charged him a whopping $30,000 for the closing. If they had taken our professional advice, they would have saved an astonishing $60,000! The moral of this story is to use a transactional attorney for the closing and to have both the buyer's and seller's prospective attorneys review the closing documents beforehand to ensure protection.

TAKING INVENTORY

A few days before closing, inventory will be taken by the buyer and seller or a third-party inventory company that both parties agree to, and they will split the cost. The purpose of this is to calculate any change in inventory since the price was agreed upon so the price can be adjusted at closing based on the new inventory count.

FURNITURE, FIXTURES, AND EQUIPMENT INSPECTION

Shortly before the closing, the buyer will also conduct a walkthrough of the business to ascertain that all of the FF&E are there as stipulated and in good working condition. If anything is missing or damaged, the sales price will need to be adjusted at closing to reflect that.

SELLER TRAINING

If the buyer needs training from the seller to run the business, the seller must let the buyer know how long they're willing to train the buyer without pay as part of the sale, which should be specified in the purchase agreement. The seller must also let the buyer know whether they're willing to continue as a paid employee or consultant and what the terms of that arrangement would be.

NONCOMPETE AGREEMENTS

We assure buyers that the seller will sign a noncompete agreement for the time frame and geographical area with the appropriate scope of precluded activities as permitted by their state.

TELL BUYERS WHAT THEY NEED TO KNOW ABOUT TRANSFERS

It is also important to address the various utilities and contractual relationships that need to involve transfers or assignments in the purchase agreement or to at least define the process that will be followed to facilitate a smooth transfer of the business. We work closely with the buyers and sellers to make sure these types of issues do not fall through the cracks and become last-minute fire drills.

LEASE

The buyer can't contact the landlord until there is an offer with escrow in place. The transfer of the lease or a new lease or sublease needs to be signed by the landlord and buyer and in place before or on closing day.

UTILITIES

The buyer will have to transfer all utility and phone accounts to their new business entity, and the day of closing will be the date of transfer. The buyer may have to put deposits down on the accounts, and the seller should receive their deposits back.

INSURANCE

Because insurance is not typically transferable (other than in a stock sale), the buyer needs to secure insurance and make sure it is active before closing. If the buyer is purchasing a business in the staffing industry, they will need to get workers' comp insurance for all employees. This can take longer than most insurances to obtain, depending on the company's workers' comp rating, so the buyer should take this into account when planning their acquisition.

TAXES

The seller is responsible for taxes up to the day of closing; after that, they are the buyer's obligation. If it is an equity deal, this needs to be expressly stated in the agreement, or the purchaser is at risk of being liable for the entire year.

In an asset sale, buyers will need to be educated on the following:

- Buyers will need to create a new business entity with a DBA (doing business as) of the business name they are buying.
- Buyers will need to get a new tax ID number, called an employer identification number, before closing.

BANK ACCOUNTS

Buyers will have to set up a business bank account, having first set up their new entity or corporation, DBA, and employer identification number (unless it's a stock sale, in which case, they may obtain the seller's bank account). If it's a stock sale for 100 percent of the business, ensure that the signatory authority has been changed to the buyer's name or that of a designee.

CREDIT CARD MACHINE

If the business takes credit cards, contact the credit card company or bank to transfer the credit card machine to the buyer's account, effective on closing day. If this is not possible, the closing documents should typically state that all income from credit card transactions from the day of closing until the transfer takes place will be transferred immediately to the buyer's account.

TELLING THE EMPLOYEES

The buyer can't talk to the employees until the seller gives written permission to do so, if the LOI or purchase agreement permits. If the business is small, the employees are told after closing. Since larger companies typically have one or two key employees involved in the transaction, the seller needs to inform the rest of the team about the sale, after closing, unless otherwise negotiated.

To avoid surprises and bad feelings, sellers and buyers should meet with the employees only after the due diligence period has elapsed and the deposit is nonrefundable.

INFORMING CUSTOMERS

To ensure a smooth transition and future success for the business, it is important that the seller introduce the buyer to as many customers as possible. But because many sellers feel uncomfortable announcing the sale of the business, especially if there is a seller financing component, the buyer may be introduced as a new partner in the business or as the new CFO, CEO, or regional manager.

In fact, many sellers and buyers agree not to tell customers that the business has been sold until the closing is complete—sometimes even months or years after the transaction.

VENDORS

Similarly to informing customers, the seller should introduce the buyer to all vendors after the sale is complete, not before.

FRANCHISES

When a franchise is put up for sale or as soon as an offer with escrow is received, the seller must tell the franchisor about the impending transfer of ownership so the franchisor can begin the qualification process. The seller normally has a right to know the reasons a buyer is not approved and should use that information when searching for another buyer.

The buyer needs to know that most franchisors require the business to be renovated at certain periods, usually after several years. The franchise agreement also often includes a clause that compels the franchisee to buy new FF&E, within reason, upon the franchisor's request. It is possible that, at inspection, the franchisor could require updates or renovations, adding to the buyer's cost.

Immediately before selling the business, franchise sellers should call their franchise representative to ensure they are up to spec on FF&E and renovation. If there are additional costs related to new furnishings or renovations, they can be folded into the sales price or split between the buyer and seller.

The buyer should also be prepared for the required training, sometimes lasting weeks, scheduled by the franchisor just before or after the inspection period. After the training, the buyer often must take a test that proves to the franchisor that they are prepared to run the business; if they do not, the transfer of the franchise is refused. We have only seen refusal happen twice in hundreds of franchise sales.

Again, education is the key to success in selling your business. If you do not properly interview and educate the buyers on all the above-mentioned items, the buyer will not be prepared, perhaps not be serious, and your deal will fall apart.

MENTORING CORNER

We see so many sellers waste precious time and resources dealing with buyers who are not qualified to buy their business. Particularly when you are dealing with first-time business buyers, it is important to make sure they have the wherewithal to qualify for financing before spending a lot of time with them. One of the greatest benefits of working with a business agent or broker is that they will do the qualifying of the potential buyer before involving you. Once you know the buyer is financially qualified, you can educate them about the other aspects of your business to prevent additional surprises down the line.

Just as it is important to have the right type of M&A advisor or broker—with the right type of experience—it is also important to have the right type of attorney—with the right type of experience—involved. Michelle expressed a concern that when attorneys are charging by the hour at closing there is a built-in conflict with their client. In this case, it is in the attorney's interest to drag out the process, renegotiate the deal, raise obstacles, and create issues that didn't exist. The nightmare example given earlier in this chapter demonstrated a transaction where the buyer apparently used the wrong attorney, both as to experience and temperament.

Just like there are good and bad M&A advisors and brokers, there are good and bad attorneys. Good attorneys, like good M&A advisors and brokers, put their clients' interests first. A good attorney will identify potential issues and misunderstandings and will work to resolve them. And, frankly, it is better to have an experienced attorney review the documentation to identify and help resolve any potential issues or misunderstandings up front, before due diligence, than to try to rectify them during the due diligence process or at closing. You do not want to complicate the due diligence process. A number of events have to happen before the end of the due diligence period, including clearing all contingencies written into the purchase agreement, or you run the risk of the buyer walking away from the deal.

It is also definitely much less expensive and time-consuming to have an experienced attorney review the documentation beforehand than to litigate over what the buyer perceives to be a breach of the purchase agreement. The purchase agreement should be complete, and anything that is important to you or the buyer should be addressed in the purchase agreement in precise terms to avoid any misunderstandings. Good attorneys with the right type of experience are trained to make sure that the purchase agreement meets those criteria.

Attorneys are like an insurance policy. They are typically not appreciated unless something goes wrong. If the deal is fair; everyone understands all the ramifications of the terms; and there are no misunderstandings about what is being sold, who does or pays what and when, and who assumes what risks, then the lawyers may not be necessary participants in the process. This, however, is rarely the case in any but the simplest of deals.

Myriad deals have included either a misunderstanding or imprecision in the documentation—which could have been avoided through proper use of experienced attorneys—where one or the other of the parties was left holding the bag, the due diligence process was unduly complicated, or the parties ended up in litigation, costing many multiples of what it would have cost to have an experienced lawyer participate in the purchase process.

The specific language used in the purchase agreement can have huge consequences. I had a client who came to me after he sold his business to discuss and plan for his future. It quickly became clear that he'd had the wrong advisors on the team that helped him through the sales process. He thought he was exiting rich with a fabulous sales price for his business. However, a review of the fine print of the purchase agreement revealed an overbroad indemnity clause under which he remained liable and responsible for the outstanding debts of the business at the time of the sale. This dramatically affected the brightness of his future planning.

Another area of potential danger is working capital, when it is included as part of the sale. Provisions in the purchase agreement defining working capital, determining how it is calculated, and potentially adjusting the purchase price due to deviations from expectations in the working capital determined during the due diligence process can be outright confusing without the assistance of a good attorney.

And then there are the provisions relating to who pays what taxes . . .

KNOW MORE TO EXIT RICH

As we learned throughout this chapter, a qualified, educated buyer is your best buyer. The more your buyer knows, the less likely they will be to back out of the deal. It's in your best interest to work with an experienced M&A advisor or business broker who can work with you to qualify and educate prospective buyers. By doing this, you will increase your chances of closing on the sale of your business.

DID YOU KNOW?

- According to *Forbes'* "22 Reasons Why the Mergers and Acquisitions Process Fails," the eighth most popular reason is because buyers are uneducated on their prospective competitors and market comparables.

- According to The Balance Small Business, educating buyers is the best way sellers can boost their client's level of confidence, thus leading to a higher chance their sale will follow through.

- According to a recent study by Stacie Grossman Bloom, confidence and positivity naturally attract followers and, therefore, are excellent traits in a leader. By equipping your buyer with the tools to feel confident in leading your business, current employees will be more likely to stay with the business.

- According to *Forbes*, when selecting the proper legal counsel for selling your business, it is important to keep in mind not only their technical skills and competence but also their ability to work with others. This will ensure that time isn't wasted on unnecessary arguments over details.

IMPLEMENTATION IS KEY

To further explore the lessons learned in this chapter, implement the following:

- Analyze and research who your buyer is so you can know how to qualify and educate them.

- Draft a financial form for prospective buyers to fill out.

- Create a buyer's interview sheet so you can qualify them on their skill sets, previous business or work experience, passions, hot buttons, and most importantly, their WHY.

- Draft an educational checklist so you don't forget to educate the buyers on all critical details.

> For a free download of Michelle's guidelines on how to educate buyers on all critical details, please visit SeilerTuckerAcademy.com.

17

Creating Emotional Connections

*"If you don't have an emotional connection
to why you are trying to accomplish your goals,
the odds are you won't reach them or will quit trying."*
—Brett Hoebel

I n most cases, people buy based on emotions, not logic. However, when buying a business, the logic must be there, especially in larger transactions. We work with a serial entrepreneur who looks at most of our businesses-for-sale inventory. He always reviews the numbers and emails an LOI immediately if the numbers meet his criteria. If the buyer accepts or comes to a meeting of the minds on price and terms, they will schedule a call, then a time and a date to meet the owners. They do not allow emotions to persuade them when buying a company. For the buyer, it's all about the numbers, the business functionality, and whether it functions on all six cylinders (the ST 6 P's).

However, other buyers are quite the opposite. Many base their decision on emotions. Of course, the numbers must make sense and meet the Buyer's Sanity Check; otherwise, the buyer will not continue the buying process on a particular business. However, even when the numbers make sense, you will want to connect the buyer emotionally to your business. If the buyer does not have a warm and fuzzy feeling and an emotional connection to your business, these types of buyers will not want to buy your company.

It's like selling a house or a car. Obviously, selling a business is much more in depth, with a lot of moving parts; however, a huge emotional connection still needs to be there. You don't (or shouldn't) buy a house unless you become emotionally involved with the house and envision where your furniture will be placed, how your yard will look, what school district your kids will attend, and what this move means to your family. You do not buy the house unless you feel as if the house will improve your quality of life. You do not buy a car unless you sit behind the wheel and take it for a spin. You imagine yourself driving your new car, picking up your friends and colleagues, and impressing them. You don't buy the car unless you feel it will improve your quality of life in some way or fashion.

The same holds true for purchasing a business. Therefore, it's important to review the five types of buyers in golden nugget 4. Sophisticated competitors and strategic turnaround buyers base their decisions mostly on logic and how the acquisition can improve their current portfolio.

First-time buyers and some of the other types of buyers must feel an emotional connection to your business. They must see themselves calling the shots and making the everyday decisions. They must feel as if the business is going to improve their quality of life in some way. Perhaps they have never owned a business before and have a desire to be their own boss. The business might give them the freedom to spend more quality time with their friends and family or to pursue a hobby. The business might allow them to afford the nicer things in life. The additional income from the business might even allow them to send their kids to college and may provide a better life for their family.

Whatever the reason, it is imperative that you know why they want to own a business and what their hot buttons are. You need to connect their WHY to your business and demonstrate that your business will absolutely help them achieve their WHY and then some. You cannot accomplish this goal if you don't know their WHY and if your business does not line up with it. Discovering and connecting the buyer to their WHY is the same with any of the five buyers. All buyers have a WHY, and it's crucial that you uncover and connect the dots; otherwise, they will not buy your company.

ENGAGING THE FIVE TYPES OF BUYERS

When selling your business, you will need to engage your buyer. As we have discussed, there are five types of buyers. Following are some tips to engage the five types of buyers and emotionally connect them to your business:

Ask the buyer to email their questions ahead of time so you can be prepared to answer them without stumbling over your answers.

Make sure that all decision makers come to tour the business. You don't want to have to show the business again due to a decision maker's absence. If not all parties can attend, reschedule.

Know when to show the business: Make sure you show it when no employees or customers are present. It is hard to concentrate on the buyer's WHY if you are distracted.

Make sure you have done everything in golden nugget 13 regarding sprucing up your business. You should not show your facility if it is not clean or if it needs repairs. Clean your business and make all repairs before the showing.

Know the proper way to tour the facility. It's best to show the buyer the entire facility before sitting down to answer questions.

Discuss different elements of your business during the tour. If you have the buyer's questions ahead of time, try to answer them while in the area that makes most sense. For example, if the buyer wants to know the flow of the hospital, explain the flow as you walk the prospect through the facility.

If the buyer is concerned with the age of your FF&E, make sure to showcase it in the best possible light. For added peace of mind, share the maintenance details with them.

Make sure to hand out brochures or marketing materials to prospective buyers. Buyers like to touch and feel things; give them whatever you can, as long as it is not proprietary.

If you own a business that sells food, beverages, or any other type of product, offer the buyer a taste or a sample. This gives them a firsthand glance (or taste) of the products you sell. They can then determine if they like your products, or they could decide to alter them.

We once sold a multimillion-dollar coffee distribution company. The seller had a beautiful facility that included a well-appointed kitchen. The seller always invited buyers to sit down at the lavishly decorated table. She would ask the buyers which type of coffee they preferred: café au lait, cappuccino, or espresso, along with their cream preference. She would demonstrate how user friendly the machines were. The aroma would fill the air as she handed them their preferred flavor in a fancy dish. The buyers felt like royalty and loved her products. They could see themselves entertaining clients in the same manner. This was impressive and left a great taste in the buyers' mouths (literally). The buyers immediately requested to buy her products. Learn from this: Don't be afraid to give away or sell some of your signature products. Even if buyers don't buy your business, they could become your next customer.

Do not discuss, disclose, or show proprietary information or processes: Buyers are like kids in a candy store; they want to know and taste everything. They will ask for customer, employee, and vendor names. Simply tell the buyer that you will be happy to divulge that information once you have an offer with escrow or at closing.

When touring the business, stay focused on answering the buyer's questions, addressing their hot buttons, and connecting your business to their WHY. Many buyers will use the tour as an actual training session on the ins and outs of your business. Do not allow the buyers to lead you into training versus touring. Remember: Training takes place after the close, not during the tour.

Allow the buyer to sit behind your desk if it's clean and does not have any proprietary information lying around. Allow the buyer to feel what it would be like to make the big-picture decisions. If the company vehicles are included in the sale of the business, allow the buyer to test drive one (just make sure it is clean and runs well beforehand). This process is quite effective if you have luxury vehicles. It doesn't have the same impact if you have a van or a truck.

We sold a luxury limousine company that had every high-end limo you could imagine. We insisted our buyers look and touch so they could experience the wow feeling along with the wow lifestyle that the luxurious limousine company provided.

Ask the buyer for input about what they would do differently or how they would improve the business. If they start providing improvements or feedback on how they would run your company, this is a good buying sign. Take it and run with it, and continue to connect your business to their WHY. If not, you need to ask the buyer for their opinion about how they would do things differently, such as what new things they would implement to improve efficiency or productivity and to reduce costs. Get them emotionally involved in running the business. If a buyer cannot see themselves running and improving your operation, they are not the right buyer. To prevent wasted time and effort, it is always better to know early on.

Ask the buyer what their biggest challenge and obstacle to overcome would be in taking over your business. They may have to learn a special skill; they may have to acquire certain licenses; they may have never managed employees before. Find out what they feel to be their biggest challenges, and see if you can implement a solution to help put their mind at ease. You have to uncover the buyer's fears and challenges in order to implement a solution that will give them peace of mind. If you can solve the buyer's perceived problems and eliminate their fears, they will buy your business. Nip any fears, concerns, and challenges in the bud early on so you can move on.

After you have completed the tour and answered all the buyer's questions, ask the buyer what their next step is in the process and move them forward. Remember: Time kills deals. Do what it takes to get the buyer to commit to the next step.

By following these steps, you will get the buyer involved in your business and connect your business to their WHY.

MENTORING CORNER

The suggestions and examples in this chapter demonstrate that while we stress the need for independent advisors or brokers to keep your own emotions in check as the seller, the opposite is true for when you as the seller deal with a prospective buyer. By allowing the buyers to see your passion and joy for your business, it can become contagious, ignite their passion, and get them more excited about buying your business.

By asking open-ended questions, buyers will become more emotionally invested in the business, and they will be able to envision themselves as the future owners.

 KNOW MORE TO EXIT RICH

In this chapter, we learned all about creating emotional connections with the buyer. When buying a business, a buyer will buy based on emotions, logic, or both. Therefore, you will need to cater your approach to the type of buyer interested in your business by following the suggestions outlined in this chapter. If your business is running on all ST 6 P's and you have your financials in order and an organized and presentable place of business, you are well on your way to impressing your buyer and making a connection with them, which will increase your chances of landing a sale.

DID YOU KNOW?

- Harvard Business School professor Gerald Zaltman says 95 percent of purchasing decisions are subconscious.

- The ability to identify and manage your own emotions and those of others can help keep emotions from influencing unrelated decisions, according to a 2013 study from University of Toronto researchers.

- According to an article on Medium.com, people buy things based on how that thing will make them feel and how they see themselves as an individual. For example, someone who considers themselves a practical, salt-of-the-earth individual is more likely to buy something cheap and without a recognizable brand because it reaffirms their self-image.

IMPLEMENTATION IS KEY

To further explore the lessons learned in this chapter, implement the following:

- Make sure your business and FF&E are clean before showing it to buyers.
- Obtain the buyer's questions before the tour.
- Know the buyer's WHY for wanting to buy your business.
- Make sure all decision makers can attend the tour.
- Ask buyers for feedback during the tour.
- Find out what the buyer's perceived concerns or fears are and address them right away.

— (18) —

How to Create a Bidding War on the Sale of Your Company

"Everything is a negotiation. Everything is a little bit of give and take."

—Lamman Rucker

The sale of your company begins with negotiations. You can't enter into a purchase agreement without first negotiating on various points. It's human nature to negotiate and to want to negotiate the best deal for ourselves. It's just how we're built. We all want to win.

However, if you don't negotiate a win for both sides, your deal will likely fall apart, or one side will perhaps move forward with a lingering feeling that they are not getting what they wanted. They did not win; therefore, they will end up frustrating the process and may still eventually back out. Granted, neither side will win on every point, which is why knowing each side's non-negotiables and negotiables is imperative.

A large amount of psychology goes into negotiations, starting with knowing your buyer. It's important to know their buying criteria, their WHY, and their most important points. Is it price, the down payment requirement, the employment agreement, or the terms of the noncompete? A good M&A agent or broker works with buyers and sellers to prioritize what the most and least important items are to each side, because not every point of contention is equal.

KNOW YOUR BUYERS AND THEIR POSSIBLE NEGOTIATING TACTICS

The type of buyer you're working with may reveal how good they are at negotiating and what's most important to them. Each type of buyer that we will discuss in this chapter will come to the negotiation with different perspectives and priorities. Let's revisit our types of buyers and identify their priorities.

FIRST-TIME BUYERS

These buyers usually make decisions based on emotions, not logic. They are nervous, skittish, and overly concerned about making a bad decision and losing their life's savings. These buyers must be handled with kid gloves, because they are typically the most likely to back out of the deal.

THE MOST IMPORTANT THINGS TO FIRST-TIME BUYERS

First-time buyers need to feel secure and that they have made a good decision.

FIRST-TIME BUYER NONNEGOTIABLES

Some things are nonnegotiable to first-time buyers:

- Showing the first-time buyer the valuation that supports the business price tag
- Seller financing
- Training
- Consulting agreement

- Noncompetes
- Reps and warranties
- Working capital

COMPETITORS AND STRATEGIC BUYERS

These buyers make decisions mostly on logic; however, some make decisions on emotions, especially if acquiring a specific business will catapult their company to the next level. This could dramatically improve their business and their quality of life.

THE MOST IMPORTANT POINTS
FOR COMPETITORS AND STRATEGIC BUYERS

Find out what they are buying and what the most important point of contention is to them, because competitors and strategic buyers buy synergies. Ask yourself whether they are buying your people, product, processes, proprietary, patrons, or profits. It's always better to negotiate when you can negotiate from a basis of strength, rather than weakness.

Remember the oil field manufacturing story? The strategic buyer was buying patrons and intellectual property; they wanted the BP contract and were willing to pay 65 percent more for 70 percent of the company, because they knew they could get an ROI from the BP contract quickly with their other company. Again, it's not always about price.

COMPETITORS AND STRATEGIC BUYERS' NONNEGOTIABLES

Some things are nonnegotiable to competitors and strategic buyers:

- Employee contracts and noncompetes
- Client contracts and master service agreements that are transferable
- Including all intellectual property
- Sufficient working capital, which includes accounts receivable and inventory
- Owner's equity

- Owner's noncompete
- Reps and warranties
- Will typically require 20-30% of seller financing, but may not agree to secure it with a personal guarantee

In most cases, they will not sign a personal guarantee on the seller financing. They will not want a seller financing personal guarantee to show on their financial statements and keep them from borrowing for future transactions.

PRIVATE EQUITY GROUPS

These buyers know their (or their family office's) buying criteria, what they're willing to pay, and the terms they must negotiate on. They will negotiate some but not much, because they have other deals lined up.

THE MOST IMPORTANT POINTS FOR PEGS

PEGs buy strictly on logic. Most PEGs are buying tenured employees, management teams, intellectual property, products, patrons, and profits. They are primarily concerned with business synergy, sustainability, potential for growth, and financials that are trending upward. PEGs require audited financials and projections.

PEG NONNEGOTIABLES

Some things are nonnegotiable to PEGs:

- Owner's noncompetes
- Employee agreements and noncompetes
- Client contracts and master service agreements that are transferable
- Including all intellectual property
- Sufficient working capital, which includes accounts receivable and inventory
- Reps and warranties
- May require 19-20% seller financing, but will not agree to secure it with a personal guarantee

TURNAROUND SPECIALIST

These buyers buy strictly on logic. Turnaround specialists (TS) buy distressed businesses that they can turn around and sell for a profit.

THE MOST IMPORTANT POINTS FOR A TS

A TS is interested in pricing and terms. They want to know how cheap they can acquire the assets, as their intent is to improve and flip it for a profit. Some will pay all cash, and many want to pay a small deposit and finance the balance.

TS NONNEGOTIABLES

Some things are nonnegotiable to turnaround specialists:

- Low price (as the business is failing and won't demand a high price)
- Seller financing terms
- Many will not sign a personal guarantee
- The ability to assign the purchase agreement or LOI

As you can see, many more factors other than price are involved in a sale. That's why knowing how to negotiate is key. Negotiating is an art, requiring skill and years of experience. Again, the most important things to know are who your buyer is, their WHY, their negotiables, and their nonnegotiables.

NEGOTIATING FROM STRENGTH

The more buyers you have, the more you can hold your ground on price and terms and negotiate the resulting sale in your favor. One of Seiler Tucker's core competencies is our ability to create bidding wars and negotiate more for our clients. We operate from a position of strength, because we have thousands of buyers of all types willing to pay top dollar (and outbid others) for great businesses operating on the ST 6 P's.

CASE STUDY: A DISTRIBUTION BUSINESS

EBITDA: $3 million
Appraised value: $9,353,000

Marketed to PEGs, strategic buyers and competitors, and sophisticated buyers
Attracted over five hundred buyers

Purchase price: $14.4 million for 70 percent of the business. The primary reason we were able to sell for more was because we had so many buyers wanting to buy the business, driving up the demand and price tag.

In this instance, we had a strategic buyer that was willing to outbid everyone else, because they were buying synergies. They were buying the patents, contracts, and even one of the partners. They knew this purchase would catapult their current business to the next level; therefore, they were not going to lose.

NEGOTIATING FROM WEAKNESS

The fewer buyers you have, the less negotiating power you have. If you don't want to entertain the buyer's price and terms, either you keep your business or you look for more buyers. In this scenario, you're not holding the gold; the buyer is. They have no connection to your business and, therefore, no reason to negotiate. Remember: There are millions of businesses for sale; the buyer will keep looking for the seller that is negotiable.

This is one of the biggest issues with trying to sell your business on your own: All your eggs are tied up in one buyer's basket, with no chance of creating a bidding war. If you lose your one buyer, you lose the ability to sell your business and you're starting from scratch.

Over 60 percent of all for-sale-by-owner business sales fail for a multitude of reasons, chief among them a lack of buyers to create competition on the seller's company will dramatically weaken the seller's position. Instead, negotiate from a position of strength by engaging an M&A or business brokerage firm that has the experience and expertise to create a bidding war on your legacy.

MENTORING CORNER

When you enter the final negotiations of the sale of your business, both you and the potential buyer have invested time and resources to get to this point. There are emotions on both sides of the table, as well as a few surprises during due diligence on both sides, which can cause more excitement or greater caution moving forward. Know what your nonnegotiables are before you get to the table, and have a neutral party or an advisor or broker help get you to the finish line.

There will generally always be a give and take needed to get to the win-win handshake. When you feel your emotions kick in, take a break and walk away before responding. It may help you process the request with a clearer head.

Sharon remembers when she was in the final negotiations for a publication of *Rich Dad Poor Dad*. There was an issue that the two parties couldn't get past. The publisher required a return for reserves of between 20 and 30 percent, which it claimed was standard for the industry. Their actual returns in the first three years of selling the book were under 1 percent, so she couldn't agree with this provision. The publisher simply didn't believe that their returns had been that low. It was very frustrating, because it was the last item to deal with before executing the deal. When Sharon decided to step away and allow her brain to focus and not allow her emotions to be in charge, she found an alternative that would work for both parties. She agreed to let them have the high reserve for returns they wanted, with the stipulation that they would true up the reserve at the end of the calendar year to the actual returns. The publisher felt comfortable with this resolution. As it turned out, at the end of the year, they had to write her a million-dollar check for the difference between the reserve they originally calculated and the actual returns. That is what we call a win-win. Both parties got what they wanted from the negotiations, and as a result the joint venture that followed generated millions of dollars of revenue and impacted millions of readers' lives.

 KNOW MORE TO EXIT RICH

In this chapter, we discussed how to create a bidding war on the sale of your business. Because a fair amount of psychology goes into negotiations, it's important to know who your buyer is. This starts with getting to know their buying criteria, their WHY, and what the most important points are to them. Working with a good M&A advisor or broker will help you present your business in the best possible light while addressing the criteria of multiple buyers to increase your chances of creating a bidding war on the sale of your company.

DID YOU KNOW?

- Successful negotiation is 80 percent preparation.
- Successful negotiators see negotiations as opportunities for both sides to win.
- According to *Forbes*, drafting the first version of any contract will most likely result in a better deal for you and allow you to have more control over negotiations.
- According to *Forbes*, creating an LOI or a term sheet, which is a less formal agreement, can expedite the process of selling your business.
- According to *Forbes*, if a seller accepts the buyer's first offer, most buyers end up with buyer's remorse because they're worried that they offered too much.

IMPLEMENTATION IS KEY

To further explore the lessons learned in this chapter, implement the following:

- Know who your buyers are.
- Determine their nonnegotiables and their negotiables.
- Have backup buyers.

To see a free training video from Michelle called "How to Create a Bidding War," please visit SeilerTuckerAcademy.com.

19

Making Your Offer Airtight

"Everything is negotiable. Whether or not
the negotiation is easy is another thing."
—Carrie Fisher

K nowing what makes an offer airtight enables you to develop the right points as you move through the process. You are much more likely to close on the sale of your business if you address certain issues and considerations during the process leading up to the sale to ensure that there are no surprises or loopholes that could halt the sale. Several different types of common agreements exist, including purchase offer agreements (POA) and LOIs.

PURCHASE OFFER AGREEMENT

POAs are commonly used with first-time buyers and in smaller transactions. They are, in effect, contracts that obligate the buyer and seller to the purchase and sale of the business, subject to due diligence by the buyer and a list of contingencies.

LETTER OF INTENT

Most of the other four types of buyers prefer to submit an LOI, because it does not commit the buyer to making the purchase or accepting specific terms. Only certain provisions of the LOI, such as confidentiality provisions, are typically binding on the parties. The LOI also usually contains binding provisions that prevent the seller from accepting other offers for a specific period, usually ninety days. However, the seller's advisors are typically not precluded from showing the business during the term of the LOI and can take backup offers. LOIs are typically used in transactions over $5 million. Although we have received LOIs for much smaller deals, we usually push back to the buyer and persuade them to submit a POA.

OBTAIN ESCROW MONEY

A percentage of the total purchase price (usually 10 percent) is posted in escrow with most POAs and LOIs. Some buyers will agree; some won't. Again, the more buyers you have in the pipeline, the more stringent you can be. PEGs may put up a thousand dollars, but they typically will not invest 10 percent escrow, because they tend to have several LOIs going at once and will not tie up funds. Depending on the type of buyer, we usually encourage our sellers not to start due diligence without escrow, which is a good faith gesture that binds the agreement. Due diligence can become expensive for both parties; therefore, you must obtain earnest money. In the purchase offer or LOI, there will be language protecting both the buyer's and seller's position regarding escrow.

NEGOTIATE AND WRITE UP A POA OR LOI

Here are things to keep in mind regarding offers:

IS IT AN ASSET OR A STOCK SALE?

The parties must identify whether the sale of the business will be an asset sale or a stock sale.

WHAT ARE THE PRICE AND TERMS?

The price and terms must be clearly stated. If there is seller financing, those terms must be spelled out, including how many years will be financed and at what interest rate. Other items to consider include whether the payments will be amortized over a longer time period and whether to balloon the note after five or ten years, as well as the amount of the payments, when they are due, and what the note is secured by.

WHAT'S THE FINANCING?

You'll want to know if the buyer is paying all cash, organizing bank financing, or pursuing seller financing. If it's all cash (unlikely), there should be no problem. If bank or SBA financing is involved, the bank will appraise the business's assets and may require using its own closing attorney and closing docs, whereas seller financing requires appropriate protection language that specifies the seller's security and terms of the seller financing note.

WHAT'S THE DOLLAR AMOUNT OF INCLUDED INVENTORY?

The offer needs to state the dollar amount of inventory (at cost) that will be included in the sale and how that value will be adjusted at closing. The offer should identify how inventory will be taken, by whom, and who pays for it. There also needs to be a cap on the inventory so the buyer can afford to pay the difference. If the buyer can't afford to pay for the excess in inventory, it needs to be seller financed.

THE FF&E LIST

The FF&E list (whether included or not included) should be attached to the POA or LOI, which will become part of the closing documents.

ACCOUNTS RECEIVABLE

You need to stipulate how much of the accounts receivable will be included and who is responsible for collections.

ACCOUNTS PAYABLE

Accounts payable needs to be stipulated as well. You'll want to know who pays what payables and whether the payables are paid from the receivables or by the seller at closing.

IS WORKING CAPITAL INCLUDED?

If working capital is part of the transaction, the contract should state a specific dollar amount. PEGs, competitors or strategic buyers, and sophisticated buyers will specify their required working capital and the formula they will use to calculate such.

LANGUAGE REGARDING THE LEASE

The POA or LOI typically includes a lease contingency, based on whether the lease will be a new lease, negotiated by the buyer and landlord, or a transfer or sublease. If it's the latter case, the POA or LOI must specify the rental rate and terms.

TRAINING INCLUDED

The POA or LOI should specify who will do the training, where it will take place, for how long, and whether it is included in the purchase or if it is paid at a certain rate.

EMPLOYMENT CONTRACT

If the sellers agree to stay on for the new owner, the purchase offer needs to identify the terms of the employment agreement. This agreement will be included in the closing documents.

NONCOMPETE

A noncompete clause is very important, because it gives the buyer peace of mind. Its terms and length need to be specified in the offer. If the seller agrees to a two-year employment agreement with the new owner, the non-compete goes into effect on the last day of that contract. Every state has different laws that pertain to noncompete agreements, so check with an experienced M&A advisor or business broker or an attorney to get the specific legal language your state requires for such agreements, or the noncompete might not be enforceable.

PRORATIONS TO BE PAID AT CLOSING

The offer needs to specify what prorations, such as rent, utilities, advertising, property taxes, or insurance (if it is a stock sale), will be paid at closing.

CONTINGENCIES

Contingencies are written to protect the buyers. They should not, however, be misused to give buyers an out or a way to simply change their mind. Buyers must be committed before signing the POA or LOI and putting up escrow. Contingencies should also protect the seller, and they must be specific.

For example, if an offer is contingent on obtaining a lease, the contingency might read like this:

> This offer is contingent upon the buyer and the landlord negotiating a lease within a 10 percent radius lower or higher than seller's current lease. The lease should not be for fewer years than seller's previous five-year lease. The buyer has five days from acceptance of this offer to schedule a meeting with the landlord. The buyer has two weeks from the acceptance date of this offer to negotiate a new lease. The seller has the right to be notified of the meeting with the landlord and has the right to attend the meeting. If the buyer and landlord can't come to terms as stated above, the buyer must provide written communication from the landlord within five business days of denial.

This contingency holds the buyer accountable to a time frame and ensures that negotiations with the landlord are fair and reasonable. There won't be as many contingencies if you allow the buyers to do the majority of their due diligence up front.

PEGs, competitors or strategic buyers, and sophisticated buyers are notorious for including boilerplate due diligence lists that are completely nonspecific and give them every possible out. We have an enormous amount of experience and success in insisting that the buyer's contingencies be specific. Most agree; some do not.

If the buyer insists on overly broad contingencies and refuses to agree to narrow the contingencies to specifics, the seller can decide whether it is worthwhile to proceed or whether the risk of wasting time and money in due diligence is just too great.

DUE DILIGENCE

Due diligence is the period during which contingencies are accepted or removed. The time frame varies, depending on the size of the transaction and the contingencies. The offer must include an expiration date for due diligence, after which the deposit is nonrefundable.

DETERMINING ALLOCATION OF PURCHASE PRICE

This is more important in larger businesses. The buyer's advisors will counsel them on choosing the allocations for the purchase price. This can become a point of contention in negotiations. The sellers must allocate the purchase price to reduce their tax liability, and it's imperative that they bring in experts to do that. If it's a C corporation, the business is subject to double taxation. Experienced tax attorneys and CPAs can help minimize the seller's exposure, and one of the ways to accomplish that is to allocate more toward goodwill and less toward tangible assets.

ACCEPTANCE DATE

If you are writing the offer, plan to have the acceptance date correspond within a short time frame from the date when you are writing the offer. The buyers might want to have their attorney review the purchase offer before signing it, so you may have to allow twenty-four to forty-eight hours for that. Similarly, if the buyer presents you with an offer to sign, you should have the same amount of time to accept or decline.

CLOSING DATE

You must identify the closing date and time frame in the closing documents. Some closings can take place in under two weeks, and some can take up to six months, depending on financing, franchise approval, and other factors, such as the contingencies. While it's possible to specify a range of thirty to forty-five days upon execution of the LOI or POA for the closing, it's not preferred. It's always better to have a specific date. You can always close before the specified date; however, if you decide to close after the closing date, both parties must agree in writing by executing an amendment to the POA or LOI.

CLOSING ATTORNEY

You need to identify the closing attorney. If permitted in the applicable jurisdiction, it's far more productive and cost effective to have an experienced attorney who represents the transaction rather than a specific party at closing. Both buyers and sellers should have their own prospective attorney review the closing docs; however, you only need one transactional attorney to close the deal.

CLOSING COSTS

While closing costs are often split between the buyer and seller, this can be negotiated. The offer should spell out who pays what.

Eliminate future disagreements between the buyer and seller and other professionals who will be involved in the closing process by negotiating and writing your POAs and LOIs so they are airtight. This is difficult on your own, especially with the emotions involved, because it's possible to get stuck on one point of contention. Therefore, it is important to know your buyers and their hot buttons and to negotiate from a point of strength.

You will save time, energy, effort, and frustration by having an experienced M&A advisor or business broker who will keep the process moving forward. In addition, the advisor will negotiate on your behalf to maximize value so you get a higher selling price for your business. For example, we have usually successfully been able to get a higher selling price than the business appraisal or than what the seller could get on their own. Our strategy of ensuring we know the players involved, their hot buttons, their strengths, and their weaknesses, as well as having a huge database of the five types of buyers, enables us to create a bidding war, which usually results in a much higher sales price for a business.

MENTORING CORNER

This is where reality sets in. The LOI or purchase agreement from the buyer becomes the outline and timeline for your sale. The more complete and precise the LOI or purchase agreement, the less likely a surprise or misunderstanding will torpedo the sale.

You'll want to review the LOI carefully to make sure it includes as many of the items shared in this chapter as possible. LOIs, also sometimes referred to as memos of understanding, are a precursor to a purchase agreement. They are not a substitute for a purchase agreement, however, and can actually add cost to the transaction. An LOI typically lays out the proposed terms for the purchase but does not bind the buyer or seller to make the purchase or sale or to accept the proposed terms. The LOI does, however, typically include binding provisions, establishing confidentiality and preventing the sale of the business to anyone else for a specific period of time—during which the buyer can perform (all or part of) due diligence or the parties can negotiate the specific terms of the purchase agreement.

Why do some buyers insist on an LOI rather than simply negotiating the terms of a purchase agreement? Generally, an LOI is used when the buyer is concerned that they do not have enough information about the business to make a rational buying decision or to intelligently craft contingencies that would protect them but still be acceptable to the seller. An LOI is also sometimes used as a tool to permit negotiation of the business terms of the deal without getting bogged down in the specific legalese of a contract, particularly with respect to the representations and warranties of the seller. A complete and detailed CIM or Due Diligence Book, provided under a confidentiality agreement, can go a long way toward giving a buyer enough confidence to go directly to a purchase agreement.

One of the most common areas of difference between the positions of buyer and seller has to do with whether the sale is an asset sale or a stock sale. If it is an asset sale, you will need to agree on how the sales price will be allocated across the assets. In addition, where the stock sale includes multiple entities, allocation between entities becomes an issue as well.

All of these issues are extremely important from a tax perspective. For instance, a sale of stock could generate capital gains at a lower tax rate for the seller, whereas selling assets may trigger depreciation recapture or ordinary income from sale of inventory, which would be taxed at higher than ordinary income tax rates. An asset sale will also leave you with any liabilities of the company, so you may need a higher sales price to net the same amount from the sale.

Make sure your tax advisor is working with you to maximize your sales price as well as to minimize your tax impact from the sale. What is optimal for you as the seller may not be so for the buyer, so there may be a need for further negotiation.

 **KNOW MORE TO EXIT RICH**

In this chapter, we learned how to make our offers airtight. By using POAs and LOIs to address any issues and considerations during the process leading up to the sale, you reduce the likelihood of any surprises or loopholes that could halt the sale of your business. When your offers are airtight, you are not only more likely to close, you are also more likely to walk away from the closing table with your desired sales price.

DID YOU KNOW?

- Some courts have ruled that offers that include acceleration clauses like "I will pay $1,000 more than your best offer" do not constitute bona fide offers.

- Most states require that you make an earnest money or good faith deposit to create a binding purchase offer.

- Deals sometimes fall through because buyers don't allocate enough time for sellers to respond to their offers. To avoid this pitfall, clarify who the accepted offer should be delivered to.

IMPLEMENTATION IS KEY

To further explore the lessons learned in this chapter, implement the following:

- If you are selling on your own, obtain a POA and LOI sample.
- Hire an experienced M&A attorney.
- Review examples of due diligence lists.
- Review the noncompete laws in your state.
- Know the negotiables and nonnegotiables for both you and your buyer.

For a free access to samples of POA, LOI, and due diligence checklists, please visit SeilerTuckerAcademy.com.

Controlling the Steps and Keeping the Players Focused

"A leader is one who knows the way,
goes the way, and shows the way."

—John C. Maxwell

Closing a deal is like being a quarterback: There are many players moving in different directions. You could be dealing with attorneys, CPAs, lenders, landlords, franchisors, and more. The seller (or their M&A advisor) must be the quarterback—in control of every step and player in the process so everything goes smoothly.

DUE DILIGENCE

The due diligence phase is all about providing all requested and approved documentation, resolving and removing every contingency in the agreement—essentially answering all of the buyer's questions and addressing all due diligence items and any concerns to the buyer's satisfaction. This process is typically overwhelming and is where most deals fall apart. Therefore it's imperative to work with your M&A advisor to gather all requested due diligence items. Expert advisors will work with their seller along with their team to gather all due diligence items from the beginning of the engagement.

Your advisor should create a data room in which to place all due diligence items and provide access to the pertinent parties. It's imperative that your advisor and attorney review all the data before giving the buyer access to the data room. Most data rooms allow the advisor to select who can review the documents and when. This process can become convoluted and will require a data room checklist to organize the files and subfiles along with what documents the buyer has permission to access. You cannot close unless every contingency has been met. Leaving a contingency unresolved can cause the deal to fall apart.

As each contingency is resolved to the buyer's satisfaction (as specified in the agreement), have your buyers sign and date a contingency-removal form that indicates their agreement to remove that contingency from the list. Another way to address contingencies is to include language in the POA or LOI that states that the buyer agrees that all contingences have been removed by the due diligence expiration date unless otherwise noted by putting in writing the failed contingencies.

Start with the contingency that will take the longest time to resolve and keep everyone on task. Be sure to address each of the following contingencies with the relevant players:

LENDER

If the sale includes commercial or SBA financing, send a copy of the signed purchase offer to the lender; don't rely on the buyer to do this. A good M&A advisor or broker will stay involved with the commercial or SBA lender until the business closes. Lenders are preoccupied with many loans, and they tend to not mention pertinent action items until the day before closing, which ultimately delays your closing.

CPA

Audited financial statements can take awhile to produce, so if any contingencies require them, get your CPA started on these immediately.

LANDLORD

Without a lease, there is no sale, but presumably, you've been renting a long time and gathered a good idea of your landlord's inclination to work with a buyer before you started the process of selling.

You, not the buyer, need to contact your landlord as soon as you execute the POA. You need to set up a meeting with the landlord and buyer to get a new lease, transfer, or sublease negotiated and approved. Some buyers feel uncomfortable negotiating with a landlord in front of the seller, so if you have a solid lease in place, make the introduction. The best M&A advisor or brokers will participate in all buyer or landlord meetings and will assist the buyers in the lease negotiations.

FRANCHISOR

Franchise owners should immediately send a copy of the purchase offer contract to the franchisor, because the franchise approval can take several weeks to months. The franchisor will set up an inspection to make sure everything is up to spec according to the franchise agreement. Once the franchisor approves the buyer, the law requires they sign a franchise disclosure document. Be aware that some franchisors require the use of their own attorney for closing; in this instance, the buyers and sellers don't have a choice and will need to use the franchisor's attorney.

ATTORNEYS

Send the closing attorneys a copy of the POA or LOI and the FF&E list so they can prepare the closing documents. However, tell them to wait to prepare closing documents until after the due diligence period is over; all contingencies have been removed; and the buyer has obtained financing, a lease, and franchisor approval. Otherwise, you'll have to pay for document prep, even if the deal falls apart.

The clock starts ticking when the due diligence period begins. When it ends, you need to have removed every contingency. Other players will not be as concerned with the clock as you are. They'll have other concerns and won't always put you at the top of the list. So be proactive and address the above contingencies early in the due diligence process.

CLOSING DOCUMENTS

Time is a resource you can't get back. When you run out of it, you're done. Once due diligence expires, you will have to review the closing documents, which will be specific to the type of sale you are engaged in. Make sure they include the following where applicable:

- Price and terms
- Bill of sale
- Seller's settlement statement
- Buyer's settlement statement
- Lease assignment or new lease
- Inventory amount
- Accounts receivable
- Accounts payable and debt: who pays what
- Working capital
- FF&E list
- Intellectual property list
- Contract and agreement list
- Noncompete agreements
- Training or employment agreements
- Promissory note
- Penalty under default
- Default procedures
- Reps and warranties
- And anything else requested by the buyer or the seller's team

We have seen many closing documents that had major errors. These days, everyone loves to cut and paste. We've seen other sellers' and buyers' names, addresses, and business names in the closing documents. Make sure that everything is correct and that everything is included. If you are using a transactional attorney, make sure each party and their respective attorneys read the closing documents prior to closing.

Time kills deals. During the sale, you will be juggling many balls in the air. Players will tend to slack, let things fall through the cracks, and drop the ball. You need to keep all the players focused and moving forward; otherwise, you will lose time, which may allow cold feet to creep in or the buyer to find another business to buy.

MENTORING CORNER

The broker or advisor's job is to highlight and use the talents of each individual participant to achieve the greatest result. If one player is off, the entire sale is affected negatively. When a problem occurs, it is the broker or advisor's job to deal with it by resolving it or improvising with some compromise or alternative action and moving on. The more years of experience, the better the broker or advisor becomes at resolving an issue without stopping forward movement in the process.

Keeping to preestablished timelines and deadlines will also keep both the buyer's and the seller's teams focused on getting to the finish line. The disclosure lists and representations and warranties are part of the closing documents. The function of the representations and warranties by the seller in the purchase agreement is to provide the buyer contractual assurances that the seller has provided them a complete picture of the business and that there are no undisclosed liabilities, lawsuits, or other surprises. The disclosure lists are intended to make sure that the buyer knows exactly what they are buying and, presumably, the risks that they are taking, at least with respect to the subject of the disclosure list.

The specific language of the purchase agreement, defining the scope of the disclosure lists and the representations and warranties, can make a huge difference in how smoothly the due diligence process goes. In many cases, the due diligence process will involve not only clearing contingencies but also putting together the disclosure lists and providing the buyer access to the underlying information so they can make their own assessment of value and risk.

continued

As we mentioned earlier, if the scope of the disclosure lists are too broad or the representations and warranties not carefully thought out, you run the risk of issues arising during the time-critical due diligence process. While you would likely be able to negotiate a workaround with a good faith buyer, you do not want to complicate the due diligence or closing process or give the buyer an excuse to back out of the deal. You and your attorney will want to fine-tune the specific language used in the purchase agreement.

In any event, you will need to provide the buyers access to the underlying items and information. This is one of the areas where having an experienced M&A advisor can really make a difference. The trick is planning, preparation, and organization from the moment you make the decision to sell your business. An experienced advisor will know the type of questions that the buyer will have about the business and precisely the type of information that the buyer will want to review to answer those questions.

The experienced advisor will also know the types of disclosure lists and representations and warranties that most buyers will demand from the seller. The process of presale valuation of the business, facilitated by your M&A advisor, will prepare you to answer many of those questions and force you to organize, compile, or identify how to access the underlying or supporting information. Having the underlying information organized and at hand and knowing where to find information will greatly facilitate keeping track of open issues and resolving each contingency within the due diligence period. For example, relatively few businesses keep all of their contracts or agreements in one place. During the presale valuation process, you can compile all of the significant contracts or agreements, or at least list where they are kept. This way, they can readily be made available to the purchaser during the due diligence process period, since during the negotiation of the purchase agreement, you would limit the scope of the contract disclosure list to the scope of your compilation or location efforts.

KNOW MORE TO EXIT RICH

In this chapter, we learned the importance of working with a trusted broker or advisor. Closing a deal is like being a quarterback: You have to consider all the different players who are moving in different directions. By working with a trusted broker or advisor, you have a better chance of being in control of every step and every player in the process so that everything goes smoothly. This, in turn, will help you achieve the best possible price on the sale of your business.

DID YOU KNOW?

- The longer a deal takes to get completed, the more likely something will occur to derail it.
- According to the Business Buyer, 50 percent of all transactions agreed to between the buyer and the seller fall apart during the due diligence stage and never close.
- The Business Buyer also states that if you do not have all your materials ready to hand over to a buyer to begin due diligence, then it can dramatically lower the possibility that your business will sell.

IMPLEMENTATION IS KEY

To further explore the lessons learned in this chapter, implement the following:

- First, set up your due diligence data room for the advisor's, attorney's, and buyer's access.
- Gather all of the buyer's required due diligence items and place in the data room. Make sure the advisors and attorneys have reviewed before releasing to the buyers.
- Obtain (or have your M&A advisor or business broker obtain) and review contingency removal forms or make sure the contingency removal is in your POA or LOI.
- Obtain and review closing docs for accuracy prior to closing.

Get a free download of Michelle's contingency removal form and data room controlled parties review list at SeilerTuckerAcademy.com

Close and Reap the Profits of Your Life's Work

"In the long run, we shape our lives, and we shape ourselves. The process never ends until we die. And the choices we make are ultimately our responsibility."

—Eleanor Roosevelt

G etting to the closing table and finalizing the sale of your business is your ultimate goal. Most deals, however, fall apart in the due diligence phase for a multitude of reasons. To avoid this, you should prepare for the close while you are in due diligence, because the two go hand in hand. If you skip any steps or let something fall through the cracks, you could lose momentum and not close. In this next section, we will cover the items that you should address or check off your closing checklist as you move closer to the closing table.

THE M&A ADVISOR OR BUSINESS BROKER

Your advisor or broker is the glue that holds your deal together. If you do not have an advisor or broker, be prepared to fill that role yourself. If you plan on taking this on alone, you should know that it is very hard to concentrate on due diligence and the closing phase and to work on or in your business while still tending to your family. If you are juggling all these balls in the air, you will want to make sure that you have a good due diligence and list of closing documents, such as the ones presented in the last chapter.

CLOSING AND TRANSFER CHECKLIST

Closing is an important time of the sale. To ensure that you cover every possible aspect, you should have a checklist of closing documents that your advisor or broker helps you prepare, such as the one given in the last chapter. In keeping with this, you will also want to make sure you have addressed each of the following, prior to closing:

- Review all closing documents
- Prepare for the transfer
- Conduct all inspections and finalizations

CLOSING DOCUMENTS

During closing you'll want to take the time to read over everything carefully. All closing documents must be reviewed one week before closing by these people:

- The seller
- The buyer
- All involved attorneys

- Some franchisors, depending on the franchisor's closing procedures, policies, and regulations
- The SBA or lender

There are usually mistakes in the closing documents. Let's face it: Attorneys are human and make mistakes. Therefore, you want to make sure that all parties involved have reviewed and approved the closing documents beforehand. You do not want to make any changes at the closing table unless absolutely necessary.

CLOSING AND TRANSFER CHECKLIST

You cannot close on the sale of your business unless the following are transferred prior to closing or on closing day. Ideally one to two weeks prior to closing, you should address all of the following that is applicable to your sale:

The Franchise or License

Sign the franchise agreement. Most franchisors will provide a letter stating they have approved the transaction and will agree upon closing. Remember, some franchisors will handle the closing and will dictate their closing attorney, time, date, and location.

The Lease

Make sure you have a written lease transfer or a new lease from the landlord. You cannot close without it. SBA lenders require ten-year leases.

Real Estate

If there is a real estate component, there may have been contingencies on obtaining a real estate appraisal. If there is a lender on the real estate, the lender's attorney will be present at closing or will want to use their own attorneys. If you are leasing your real estate to the buyer, make sure the closing attorney or your attorney draws up a lease for you and the buyer. And if you are providing seller financing, make sure that your attorney has tied the lease to the buyer's performance regarding seller financing security.

Vehicles

The attorneys will need to see the title of all vehicles prior to closing.

Bank Accounts

Make sure the buyers have opened their bank account prior to closing.

Credit Card Machines

Ensure that the credit card machine is transferred to the buyer so that all money deposited after closing deposits into the buyer's account on the day of closing.

Utilities

Make sure all utilities will be in the buyer's name at closing.

Phones

Make sure all phone lines or numbers will be in the buyer's name at closing.

Contracts

Make sure all customer and employment contracts are transferable to the buyer and everything transfers over without any issues. Do this at least thirty to ninety days before closing.

Vendors

This is part of accounts payable. Pay all vendors or accounts payable that are associated with collected accounts receivable out of the proceeds of the business and assist the buyers with setting up their own accounts with all vendors. Remember, accounts payable or vendors associated with accounts receivable will typically be paid by the buyer, unless otherwise negotiated.

Licenses

Many states and counties require certain licensing. One small parish in Louisiana, for example, insists that all buyers go to a council meeting and speak to the board to obtain the required license to start or purchase a business. If you are selling a contracting business or any other specialized business that requires a license, make sure the buyers have procured the appropriate licenses to run the business. This is especially true if the buyer is obtaining an SBA loan. The SBA requires that the buyer have all appropriate licenses before transfer of the loan money and closing. A good M&A advisor or broker will assist buyers with obtaining all their licenses and everything else required on this checklist.

INSPECTIONS AND FINALIZATIONS BEFORE CLOSING

Before closing, there will be some inspections and finalizations done by the buyer and seller and their teams.

FF&E

Conduct a walk-through so the buyer can inspect all furniture, fixtures, and equipment to make sure everything is there and in working order before you close.

Inventory

As we previously mentioned, the buyer and seller need to take inventory a few days before closing or on the day of closing. The inventory dollar amount needs to be sent to the closing attorney so they can adjust the settlement statement, if necessary. Keep in mind that, depending on the size of the company, inventory might take days. Therefore, if it is a large company, you will need to address this well before the closing date.

We sold a large manufacturing company that had approximately $2 million in inventory. The buyer or seller hired a third-party inventory company that took over a week, working about twelve hours a day, to complete the inventory. After completing the inventory, we had to go back to both the buyer and the seller, because the inventory was short and the payables were higher than anticipated. At that point, we had to renegotiate the deal. The seller gave $350,000, the buyer gave $350,000, and we also contributed from our fees to get the deal done. These are the components in a transaction that can affect the agreed-upon selling price, and everyone needs to be willing to compromise if the deal is going to close.

Prorations

All prorations need to be agreed upon and sent to the attorney to finalize the settlement statement. These can get down to the wire, because everyone is waiting on payoff letters, balance sheets, P&Ls, and so on.

Accounts Receivable

You will need to provide a final accounts receivable report to the buyer and their representative. Note that the business sales price changes as accounts receivable increases or decreases.

Accounts Payable

You will need to provide an updated accounts payable report that corresponds with the uncollected accounts receivable to the buyer and their representative. This can become quite complicated.

We sold a medical staffing company that had SBA financing. The POA specified that the accounts payable associated with accounts receivable be paid by the buyer from the accounts receivable. SBA requires the seller's line of credit to be paid off at closing. Therefore, the closing attorney paid off the line of credit out of the proceeds of the sale on closing day, and the buyer paid $40,000 to the sellers out of their line of credit and paid the sellers the remaining $50,000 upon collecting the accounts receivable.

It's common practice for buyers to require a certain amount of the proceeds be held in escrow for any accounts payable that fell through the cracks.

Gift Certificates and Prepaid Events

Gift certificates and prepaid events must also be finalized before the closing and communicated to all parties involved. The seller must provide the buyer or the buyer's representative with a ledger of all prepaid gift cards that have not been redeemed and prepaid events that have not yet occurred. There are different ways to handle this; however, the most common way is to allocate the amount of unredeemed gift cards or future events. This amount is added to the settlement statements and credited to the buyer. In some cases, all parties will agree to escrow the said amount for a designated period in order for the cards to be redeemed and the events to occur. If neither happens, the funds could be returned to the seller.

Revenues on Closing Day

Some sellers will allow the buyer to have all the money that came in on the day of closing. Some sellers will not, and the buyer gets all money the day after closing. It really depends on the time that you are going to close. If you are going to close early morning and go back to the business with the buyer, the buyer should have the revenues for that day. If you are closing late in the afternoon, the seller should have the proceeds for that day.

Locks and Keys

Change the locks or get additional keys made. In some cases, the buyer wants the locks changed. If you are the landlord, you also have the right to keep a key. If you are seller financing, you have the right to keep a key, especially if you own the building.

THE DAY OF THE CLOSING

Closing day is the moment you've been planning for, most likely for years. Emotions run high on both sides, so you will want to be sure you are prepared and have the following in order before you close:

CLOSING LOCATION AND TIME

Make sure everyone has agreed on the place and time to close so all parties are present. Don't be surprised if the closing date gets pushed back; this is typical due to last-minute issues that arise.

DETERMINE WHETHER YOU WILL HAVE AN IN-PERSON OR A VIRTUAL CLOSING

Some closings are in person, and some are virtual. In-person closings typically involve the closing attorneys and, in some cases, the lender's legal counsel. These days, many closings are virtual, through Zoom, Skype, or phone.

Regardless of which option you choose, in most cases, a notary will need to be at the closing to notarize specific closing documents.

ACCURACY OF DOCUMENTS

Carefully review all closing documents (especially settlement statements) for accuracy.

FUNDS

In larger transactions, the funds are usually wired to the escrow of the closing attorney. This attorney ensures that all debt or accounts payable, closing costs, and so on are paid. Upon receipt of those items, the attorney will wire the remaining funds to the seller. In smaller transactions, the buyers may bring a cashier's check made out to the seller or the closing attorney.

DRY CLOSING

There are times when we will conduct a dry closing. A dry closing means that the buyer or seller have closed on the sale of the business; however, money has not changed hands. This does not happen often, but sometimes it's necessary.

We once sold a multimillion-dollar company, and the buyer was adamant about a particular closing date because he wanted the millions that were pouring in from a big job. The seller was motivated to sell because of a pending divorce. Unfortunately, the buyer's lender suffered a heart attack and was out and could not close on the funds, even though the loan was approved. As a result, both parties agreed to a dry closing. The buyer ran the business with the seller, and they received funding within thirty days.

TRAINING

Once you've closed on the sale of your business, it isn't time to wrap up. It's time to train. Training the buyer is important, because you want to make sure you leave your employees and customers in good hands. And if you are seller financing, you especially want to make sure the buyer is well trained. Train them first, then celebrate and take your much-deserved vacation.

GLITCHES

The steps in this book certainly make the due diligence and closing process sound easier than it is. We have sold hundreds of businesses and franchises. In all our experience in selling businesses, we have never had a closing without problems arising.

We always ask our team the same question: "When does an M&A advisor or business broker's job really begin?" Many will reply, "It's when you set up your first appointment with the seller." Many others will say, "It's when you sign the engagement agreement." And some will say, "The advisor's job begins when you locate a buyer or when you sign an LOI or POA." You may be surprised to hear that all those answers are incorrect.

Of course, our job includes all those steps. But our job *really* begins when we have a business under contract and the deal starts to unravel. That is when the job of an M&A advisor or business broker truly starts, and they work as the glue that holds your deal together.

If you are handling the sale of your business, be prepared for many issues and obstacles along the way. So much can go wrong that it's impossible for us to include everything that might interrupt or impede the closing of the sale of your business. The key is to dot the i's and cross the t's every step of the way. You must have tremendous intuition, which comes from experience, to know what is going to happen before it happens. Once the unthinkable occurs, it is usually too late to address and resolve the issues. Not everyone can put Humpty Dumpty back together again. Doing this, however, has become our specialty, thanks to our long and varied experiences.

If you find yourself ready to make a major change in your life by selling your business but you do not feel you have the expertise, time, or resources to successfully sell your company yourself, we understand. Selling your business is extremely difficult. You have to concentrate on getting your business to run on all cylinders by using the ST 6 P's, obtaining a valuation, packaging the business for sale, marketing the business, qualifying buyers, assisting with lending, negotiating the offer, reviewing counteroffers, conducting due diligence, and monitoring and controlling every aspect through the closing phase, all while working on your business and still tending to your family. We get it. It's a lot!

We know this because, at Seiler Tucker, we have sold hundreds of businesses, all while operating our businesses and tending to our families. We have done all these tasks, and we know how much work and effort it takes. If you feel you are up to the challenge, carry on. However, if you are feeling completely overwhelmed at the prospect of taking all of this on yourself, hire an expert!

MENTORING CORNER

In her experience as a mentor, Sharon has found additional issues that may need to be addressed prior to closing as well as finalized at closing.

Following are a few other things that should be dealt with prior to closing (albeit typically taken care of during the course of the due diligence process):

- If your business is structured as a corporation or LLC, you should have a corporate resolution or resolutions from the LLC members authorizing the sale.

- Where intellectual property is part of the transaction, written assignment documents transferring rights to the IP are typically required, typically provided to the buyer for review prior to closing. In the case of patents, trademarks, and copyrights, the assignment documents must be suitable for recording with the patent and trademark or copyright office (typically by the buyer after closing).

- It is also not uncommon, particularly with respect to technology companies, for a portion of the purchase price to be placed in escrow to protect the buyer from breaches of your representations and warranties, or specific contingencies. If this is the case with respect to your business, prior to closing you will need an escrow agreement in place with a "trusted third party"—the escrow agent—that clearly and explicitly lays out the criteria for releasing escrowed funds to you.

While it may seem obvious, if the purchase agreement calls for you to stay involved with the business under the terms of a consulting, management, or employment agreement, or calls for a noncompetition or nonsolicitation agreement that limits your postsale activities, you should insist

continued

on receiving copies as early as possible, and in any case, far enough in advance of closing to permit your attorney to review them and negotiate any necessary changes. The last thing you want is to be surprised by the terms of ancillary agreements and having to delay closing until they can be reviewed and any issues resolved.

》》》

In addition, there are items that need to be addressed, **and possibly valued**, at the time of closing. Depending on the nature of the business being sold and the terms of the purchase agreement, there may be a few other items to "finalize." These include:

- **Work in Process.** Where it is relevant, the purchase agreement typically specifies who will handle completion and warrants the support of existing projects, and how the revenues from those products will be distributed. The buyer and seller will often take inventory and determine the state of the work in process a few days before closing or on the day of closing and adjust the settlement statement accordingly.

- **Working Capital.** As mentioned earlier, the purchase agreement may require that working capital be transferred as part of the sale. Generally, the purchase agreement will include an agreed-upon figure for working capital, which is later reconciled—"trued up"— against actual numbers. Occasionally, a revision of the agreed-upon figure will be required at closing, although a final "true up" commonly occurs 60 to 120 days after closing.

- **Allocation of Purchase Price.** If the transaction is an asset sale, for tax purposes, you may also have to finalize an allocation of purchase price among the various assets purchased.

》》》

In summary, "You don't know what you don't know." This particular saying is quite applicable when you are selling your business. No doubt no one knows your business as well as you do. You are an expert at selling your products or services. However, since you are not in the business of selling businesses, you may not be the best quarterback for selling your business, and your business may suffer if you try to take on this new role. Do yourself, your business, and your family the favor of having the experts who sell businesses every day join your team.

If you have been working with the right type of M&A advisor or business broker and have gone through the details of the purchase agreement with an experienced attorney, most issues will have been brought to light and resolved during the course of negotiating the purchase agreement and the subsequent due diligence by the buyer.

We have already discussed putting together an information package and collecting materials on the business as soon as you make the decision to sell and that the guidance of your M&A advisor or business broker (and sometimes your attorney) in assembling that package can be invaluable. For example, the purchase agreement will often call for you, as the seller, to provide disclosure lists of specific information and to assert (in legalese, "represent and warrant") that those lists are complete as of the date of closing. These lists often include all FF&E, contracts, or agreements to which your business is a party, and intellectual property held by your business. A well-thought-out information package will give you a head start in complying with due diligence requests that would otherwise delay the closing.

In addition, the buyer will often also request representations (reps) and warranties relating to specific items on the list. For example, a buyer might request a guarantee that the FF&E list includes all of the FF&E owned by your company, that all of the items are in good working condition and not in need of repair, and that FF&E conveyed are adequate to continue conducting the business in the same manner as before the sale.

What's the danger in that representation? What if some of the equipment needed repair as part of normal maintenance or there was broken-down office equipment owned but no longer used by the company sitting in some storage room? If that was the case, you would be in breach of that warranty. Presumably, the issue would be discovered during due diligence, and a good faith buyer would agree to a workaround, but you do not want to complicate the due diligence or closing process or give the buyer an excuse to back out of the deal. It would be in your best interest if a change in the language of the purchase agreement was negotiated before the due diligence process so that it called for a list limited to FF&E that you actually

continued

used in the normal course of business and a rep and warranty that did not include the "not in need of repair" language. This is where a good attorney with the right type of experience comes in.

Other common disclosure lists requested from the seller relate to contracts or agreements to which the business is a party and to intellectual property held by the seller. As with the FF&E list, the specific language of the purchase agreement describing the scope of the lists can be important, both in the due diligence process and for liability under the purchase agreement. For example, the term *intellectual property* includes more than just patents and registered trademarks. It also includes, for example, know-how, trade secrets, and common law (unregistered) trademarks.

A complete listing of those items can be a Herculean—if not impossible—task, but the omission of equipment, a trade secret, or trademark from a supposedly complete list can have consequences down the line if the buyer ever needs to enforce their rights with respect to that "missing" property. It is best that the language of the purchase agreement be negotiated prior to due diligence and closing to limit the scope of the list so that these and similar issues can be avoided.

 KNOW MORE TO EXIT RICH

This chapter was all about preparing for the close. Taking the time to properly prepare for the close will help you reap the greatest possible reward on the sale of your business. Because most deals fall apart in the due diligence phase, we encourage you to prepare for the close while you are still in the due diligence. By following the closing checklist we provided, you will be less likely to skip any steps or to let something fall through the cracks, thereby increasing your chances of making it to the closing table.

DID YOU KNOW?

- To truly leave behind a lasting legacy, you need to start planning in your fifties. Unfortunately, most people do not start until they are in their sixties.

- According to Close, Mark Cuban's success comes from selling his startup, Broadcast.com, for $5.7 billion to Yahoo! in 1999.

- Ander Michelena and his partner Jon Uriarte saw a need for an online venue for ticket holders to sell extra tickets and passes when they couldn't make it to the event. After seven years of building their market, they sold their company, Ticketbis, eBay to StubHub for $165 million.

IMPLEMENTATION IS KEY

To further explore the lessons learned in this chapter, and if selling on your own, implement the following:

- Create your closing and transfer checklist and ensure everyone follows it.

- Make sure all the points of the closing docs are included and are accurate.

- Ensure everyone reviews the closing documents.

- Make sure the buyer has all necessary transfers.

- Ensure the money is wired or the buyer brings a cashier's check.

Get your free sample of Michelle's closing and transfer checklist
at SeilerTuckerAcademy.com.

Build to Sell

"Your work is going to fill a large part of your life, and the only way to be truly satisfied is to do what you believe is great work. And the only way to do great work is to love what you do."

—Steve Jobs

After reading this book, you may be thinking, *I would love to sell my business, but I am nowhere close to having a sellable business* or *I'm not ready now but would love to sell in the future.* And that's okay. However, remember that people don't plan to fail; they fail to plan. We don't want to see any business owner fail!

Our purpose in writing *Exit Rich* was to enlighten business owners and provide insights on how and when to sell their business. As we discussed in golden nugget 2, timing is everything. If you don't get the timing right, you could end up being one of those businesses that doesn't sell, and you could lose everything you have worked so hard for, which would be disastrous.

It's our passion and mission to help business owners fix and grow their business and build to sell for their desired price tag. At Seiler Tucker, we are committed to improving and rewriting the unfortunate statistics that sellers face: Eight out of ten businesses will not sell for a multiple of reasons, and 70 percent of businesses will go out of business after being in operation for ten years. These are startling statistics that all business owners face.

Unfortunately, no business owner is immune to going out of business. Many owners are blind to the statistics and think it will never happen to them. Just remember that businesses go through stages from their birth to their death. Your business could be in its prime, and before you know it, it ends up in the senior citizen stage and on life support due to unforeseen circumstances or the result of poor decision making.

Many of these grim statistics are the fault of business owners, because most of the mistakes that owners make can be avoided if they align themselves with an expert to guide them and keep them from stepping in landmines. That's why it's imperative to follow the GPS Exit Model, to operate on all ST 6 P's, and to keep your eyes on your current location and destination and adjust your sails along the way. Many of the examples that follow show you what can happen when you follow the ST 6 P's and engage the proper business authority to help you stay on track and assist you with building your multimillion- or billion-dollar company to sell, all while following the GPS Exit Model.

STORIES OF BUSINESS LIFE EXPECTANCY

FROM BIRTH TO DEATH

A large industrial staffing business hired us to sell their company. The business was doing great, with offices throughout the United States generating an EBITDA close to $3 million. We had hundreds of hungry buyers that wanted to purchase a staffing company. Many buyers were strategic buyers or competitors and willing to outbid others. This company could have sold in the $20 to $30 million range. However, during the engagement process, the owner made poor and self-destructive decisions. He left his wife for his childhood sweetheart, took his eyes off his business, and traveled around the world.

His staffing company then suffered a catastrophic injury. His company had lost its workers' comp carrier but nevertheless continued to operate as an industrial staffing business, resulting in the loss of one of its largest clients. This business went from high cash flow to losing money overnight—so much so that they ended up filing for chapter 11 bankruptcy.

Our buyer (a competitor buyer) was under contract and initially agreed to pay millions. In the end, he ended up buying the company for $1.2 million in bankruptcy court. That money went to pay creditors, so the seller ended up with nothing. Worse yet for the seller, the $1.2 million did not cover all outstanding taxes and debt, so he's still on the hook for the remainder of the company's liability, because as most business owners do, he involved his personal assets in the business by signing personal guarantees.

Unfortunately, these stories are more prevalent than you would imagine. In this example, not only the seller lost; his family, employees, clients, and vendors all lost as well. Many say that the buyer won (he paid a lot less for the business), but that's not true. We got the buyer approved by the bankruptcy court as the "stalking horse," and he operated the staffing business under a management agreement at a loss for months while the company was in chapter 11. In addition, the buyer spent a lot of money on top of the $1.2 million for damage control and to rebrand and rebirth the company. It cost a lot of money, time, energy, and resources to fix and grow the company, especially since the business's reputation had been damaged.

We don't want the above scenario to ever happen to any business owner. When a business dies, it doesn't only take the business's assets to the grave; it typically takes the family assets as well. Therefore, it's imperative to act prudently, align yourself with an expert growth advisor, and build your business to sell for your desired price while it is thriving and attractive to prospective buyers.

FROM NEAR DEATH TO REBIRTH

A first responder graphics company called us about selling their business. We asked the owner, "Why do you want to sell?" His reason was, "I don't have the business acumen to grow the company." He said, "My wife and I are working fourteen hours a day from our home office. We have one employee, we are beyond exhausted, and it's putting a strain on our marriage."

As we continued to ask him questions, he shared, "Our product is in demand, and we provide the highest quality art, craftsmanship, and service in our industry. But we can't keep up with the demand and are turning down over a thousand clients a year."

When he said that, a light bulb went off: This company is printing money, but they are not operating on all the ST 6 P's to keep up with demand.

Most business problems are not due to having too many clients. It's usually the opposite problem—not having enough clients—that is the issue. One of the biggest deficits in fixing a business is getting enough customers to purchase the company's products and services. In this case, they were functioning well with one of the ST 6 P's, patrons, because they had more than they could service. Even though this sounds like a good problem to have, and it is, the hidden issue with having too many clients is that their brand was rapidly diminishing due to their inability to provide the excellent service and outstanding customer experiences they were known for, because they were lacking in the other P's.

The owner's perceived issue, a lack of business acumen, was the symptom, not the problem. Let's look at the ST 6 P's in his situation and identify the real problems:

People

The business essentially had no people. It was him (the owner), his wife, and one employee. Therefore, he had no business; he had a job.

Product

The business delivered a high-end quality product to a niche market—first responders, with little to no competition—and their product was in high demand.

Process

The business had no people and no process. They were too busy taking orders, designing or printing graphics, scheduling installs, installing, dealing with clients, putting out fires, and so on. Due to the lack of time and being overwhelmed, they could not focus on every other aspect of their business.

Proprietary

They did not have much that was proprietary, other than their brand and an unparalleled quality of art, installs, and service. However, their brand was at risk because they were struggling to maintain their level of service due to a lack of people and process.

Patrons

They had lots of patrons. According to the owner, they were turning down thousands of clients per year. The problem was they could not service them because they weren't running on all cylinders or ST 6 P's.

Profits

They operated on a good profit margin and were making money. Therefore, unlike many businesses that are losing money, they were making profits. Remember: He called us to sell his company because he didn't think he had the business acumen to grow it to the next level. In reality, he was not lacking business acumen. He was too busy working in his business rather than on it, which is why he couldn't see the forest for the trees.

We always say, "When you're in the middle of the fog, it's foggy." His business was not sellable because they would be selling a job, not a business. Once you took the husband and wife out of the business, there *was* no business. Furthermore, they were working from home and did not have a location. They also made a fatal mistake: telling their one employee that they were selling and/or closing the business. That employee did what most would and found another job. If we were able to sell the job of the owners, by the time the proceeds paid their debt, taxes, and commissions, there would be nothing left for the owners to live on. They would have to become employees rather than employers, which is never a viable solution for owners after being self-employed for decades.

During our conversation with this owner, we noticed something. Even though he sounded distraught over his business, he still sounded passionate about his company. He's an artist and had been doing art since he was six years old. He loved his business, his art, and his clients. While some of his clients were firefighters, he found himself putting out fires daily. Unfortunately, that's what happens when business owners become stuck in the day-to-day operations and stop doing what they love. In spite of this, he still had the seventh P, passion. Passion is what we look for when partnering with business owners to build their business to sell for millions. If there is no passion for the company, we would likely walk away or build their company by being 100 percent in charge.

Because both husband and wife had so much passion for their business, we were able to find a viable solution for all parties. The solution, at the time, was not to sell the business. This couple was upside down in debt, and they could not afford to close their business, especially since they had a second mortgage on their family home. We recognized the opportunity and offered to partner with them as we began our process to fix, grow, and build to sell their business for their desired sales price of $50 million. We invested money in their business and brought in another partner who had a similar (but different) business, which added resources. We also leased a building, hired employees and a COO, leased new equipment and vehicles, and started implementing the ST 6 P's. Our partners are now operating a business, not a job!

It turns out the owners did have the business acumen to grow. He and his wife have created and implemented many brilliant ideas to catapult our company to the next level, because they are visionaries. Their business acumen was hidden by the day-to-day demands of a business that was not operating on all ST 6 P's.

The moral of this story is selling your business now is not always the best solution. You must, therefore, align yourself with an expert to determine if selling or building to sell is the best option for you and your family.

FROM HEALTHY ADULT TO A NEAR-DEATH EXPERIENCE

We once worked with an advertising agency that wanted to sell their business. They were more advanced than most business owners because they had done a great job of following the GPS Exit Model. They had a desired sales price and time frame and, most importantly, knew their WHY. What they did not know was their current valuation. As a result, they were not operating on all the ST 6 P's. They were a boutique advertising agency, first mentioned in golden nugget 9, that specialized in advertising and marketing for casinos.

The problem was they only had five casinos. Talk about customer concentration. If they lost a casino, they would suffer financial hardship.

Let's take a closer look at their ST 6 P's:

People

They had lots of talented employees and managers. Their only people issue was they had a lot of highly paid ad executives, and if they lost any one of their five casinos, they would be upside down in employee overhead.

Product

Their service was in demand. However, it was very niche and at risk of becoming replaced as casinos brought in their own in-house ad agencies.

Process

They had efficient and productive processes in place that were well documented. In addition, employees were well trained on the processes and procedures.

Proprietary

They did not have anything proprietary other than their brand specialty of marketing for casinos. They had no contracts in place, because the casinos refused to sign them. This was a huge problem. Contracts are important; a buyer will almost certainly want them to ensure future cash flow.

Patrons

They were not diversified and had huge customer concentration tied up in only five casinos. Therefore, if they lost one or two casinos, they would be out of business.

Profits

Despite being profitable, the company's profit margins were slim and at risk, due to the high employee overhead.

Out of the ST 6 P's, they were only truly functioning on three: people, process, and profits. Their product was at risk of being replaced with in-house ad agencies, and they did not have enough patrons or anything proprietary.

We valued their business at $5 million; however, during our valuation process, they lost two casinos. Their EBITDA drastically decreased overnight, but their overhead stayed the same, because they had to keep their highly paid, talented employees to maintain the other three casinos. Their business suddenly became worth much less than our $5 million valuation, and the owners were no longer on track to meet their exit goals.

We helped them refocus by merging them with another ad agency that came to us to sell. This agency had the opposite problem. They had lots of diversified clients but not enough talented employees to service them, and they were having trouble finding the right employees. Therefore, we worked our magic and partnered them with our casino advertising company. The synergies aligned, and this partnership became a marriage made in heaven. They are now on track to sell for even more than their desired sales price of $15 million.

Their GPS Exit Model

- End game or desired sales price: Sell the business for $15 million

- Current valuation: $5 million

- WHY: Help his wife fight her debilitating disease and find a cure; this is a very powerful WHY

- Time frame: three to five years

- Life plan to achieve their end game: (Our plan) increase EBITDA from $1,392,000 to $2,800,000

- Precise plan to increase earnings: (Our plan) partner with a business owner in the same industry that is struggling in different areas and not a competitor

- Benefits: Increase revenues, add congruent revenue streams, diversify, and expand client base

- Share life plan: He shared his life plan and enlisted the brain trust of the business authorities that could assist in accomplishing his end game

- Result: We sold the business for more than his desired $15 million to a strategic multimillion-dollar buyer that already existed in our buyer pool. Both companies benefited from this merger, and it worked because the ad agency casino owner still had the seventh P, passion.

>>>

It is our sincere hope that this book has helped you feel better prepared to sell your business. In this last chapter, we wanted to share some additional examples to help illustrate these topics:

- When to sell
- When not to sell
- When to build to sell
- How healthy businesses can instantly die
- How putting out fires burns business acumen
- How owners' decisions can cause self-destruction and business destruction
- How not operating on the ST 6 P's can ruin a business
- How not following the GPS Exit Model® can be detrimental for the owner and their family
- And, most importantly, if you don't have the seventh P, passion, you can't build to sell

If you hire the wrong advisor or broker, it could cost you your business, your livelihood. And if you go it alone, you could run into similar issues. We wrote this chapter to open your eyes so you can start the process and determine the best strategy for you and your family. As you have read this book, we're sure that the task of selling or building your business to sell sounds daunting. Throughout this book, we have done our best to create your step-by-step blueprint to follow to ensure the successful sale of your business and to help you achieve all of your financial dreams.

For additional guidance, we invite you to visit our website at
www.seilertucker.com, call us at 877-853-4227, and
explore the bonus nuggets in the appendix.

MENTORING CORNER

In the example titled "From birth to death," it appears that the original owner of the industry staffing business ended up on the hook for the company's liabilities, that he was either forced to give a personal guarantee to creditors or he failed to lay a proper foundation for the success of his business, because he did not set the business up as a limited liability entity corporation.

In the example titled "From healthy adult to a near-death experience," Michelle described acquiring resources to build her ad agency clients' businesses to put them in a better position for sale using an alternative to spending money. The first ad agency had personnel resources but lacked clients. The second agency had the resources that the first agency needed, and the first agency could supply the personnel resources that the second agency needed. By merging, each of the respective ad agencies, in effect, traded equity in their business to the other in return for the resource they needed. This is a perfect illustration of the principle of using other people's resources to build a business rather than attempting to sell the equity.

We are advocates for the expert counsel of experienced professionals in business. Whether a tax accountant, intellectual property attorney, or member of your business advisory counsel, enough cannot be said for working with people who have been where you want to go and successfully achieved your goals for themselves or on behalf of others. In the business world, there are a lot of individuals that talk about how to do things the "right" way that unfortunately don't have the experience to back up their advice. The insights in this book are the result of successful experiences by Seiler Tucker in working with their clients. We are honored to have made *Exit Rich* available to you. The steps outlined in this book are not theories. They are proven models for achieving the greatest value for your business, and we recommend that you follow them closely for the greatest possible success.

APPENDIX

BONUS NUGGETS

1

The Road Map to Selling Your Business

Going Alone, the Road to Selling Your Business

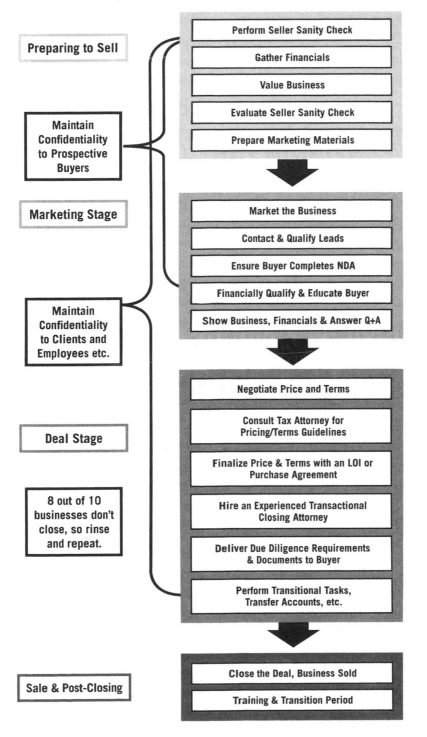

Preparing to Sell

Perform Seller Sanity Check

Gather Financials

Value Business

Evaluate Seller Sanity Check

Prepare Marketing Materials

Maintain Confidentiality to Prospective Buyers

Marketing Stage

Market the Business

Contact & Qualify Leads

Ensure Buyer Completes NDA

Financially Qualify & Educate Buyer

Show Business, Financials & Answer Q+A

Maintain Confidentiality to Clients and Employees etc.

Deal Stage

Negotiate Price and Terms

Consult Tax Attorney for Pricing/Terms Guidelines

Finalize Price & Terms with an LOI or Purchase Agreement

Hire an Experienced Transactional Closing Attorney

Deliver Due Diligence Requirements & Documents to Buyer

Perform Transitional Tasks, Transfer Accounts, etc.

8 out of 10 businesses don't close, so rinse and repeat.

Sale & Post-Closing

Close the Deal, Business Sold

Training & Transition Period

Seiler Tucker Resources

Free Book Membership

Every purchase of *Exit Rich* includes a lifetime book membership. Through this membership, you will receive additional proven strategies and nuggets such as MST's deep dive training videos, case studies, document downloads, sample offers, LOI's, due diligence list, closing docs, and more!

seilertucker.com/freemembership

Free Newsletter

Members will receive a monthly newsletter highlighting major M&A news topics, an array of case studies, industry updates, available acquisitions, and much more.

seilertucker.com/newsletter

Webinars

Seiler Tucker webinars provide exclusive insight into what's hot and what's not in the business realm. You will learn what buyers are looking for in a business, how to operate utilizing the "ST 6 P's Method," how to create synergies that will attract many buyers, how to create a bidding war for your business, creative financing strategies, and much more.

seilertucker.com/webinar

Seiler Tucker Resources

Club CEO's Access

As the leading authority on buying, selling, fixing, and growing businesses, Michelle has seen it all during her 20 plus years in the trenches. In addition, Seiler Tucker has sold over a thousand businesses and fielded calls from thousands of business owners before and during this unprecedented time. Michelle has her finger on the pulse of exactly what you need to know and do right NOW to not only survive but thrive and build a sustainable, scalable, and sellable business, so when you're ready, you too can "Exit Rich."

seilertucker.com/clubceos

Build to Sell™ Blueprint

In the Build to Sell™ Blueprint, Michelle Seiler Tucker will guide you step-by-step through your journey of how to build a successful business to sell for your desired exit price. She will illustrate what it takes to create the underlying foundation and build your organization structure on the "ST 6 P's Method" to ensure your business is profitable, sustainable, scalable, and sellable.

seilertucker.com/course

Mastermind

Work directly with Michelle Seiler Tucker to learn the insider's trade secrets and the do's and the don'ts of buying & selling businesses. Learn the power of negotiations of synergies and how to create a bidding war on your business. Learn how to sell for your price and your terms. Dive deep into the golden nuggets, live hot seats, and Q&A sessions to better understand how to scale and "Exit Rich."

seilertucker.com/mastermind

Hire Michelle Seiler Tucker

Hire Michelle Seiler Tucker to sell your business or partner with her to build to sell your business!

seilertucker.com/hiremichelle

Mastermind with Michelle and Sharon to Build a Sustainable, Scalable, and Sellable Business

Michelle Seiler Tucker

- Leading Authority on Buying, Selling, Fixing, and Growing Businesses
- Certified M&AMI, CSBA, CM&AP, CBB
- 20 Years Experience selling over 1,000 Businesses
- The USA's Top Closer
- Two-time #1 Best-Selling Author
- International Keynote Speaker
- Hosts "Exit Rich" Podcast

Sharon Lechter

- New York Times Best Selling Author and Co-Author of *Rich Dad Poor Dad*
- Licensed CPA for 35 years
- Wrote 4 bestselling *Think and Grow Rich* series books with the Napoleon Hill Foundation
- Advisor to two U.S. Presidents on financial literacy
- International Keynote Speaker
- Driving force behind 3 global brands

Michelle and Sharon have teamed up to co-author *Exit Rich* and provide a unique Mastermind Event. Learn in-person from two of the leading authorities in building a sustainable, scalable, and sellable business. You will be immersed in a personalized think tank, chart your course of success personally and professionally, take part in guided strategy development, and much more!

For more information visit
seilertucker.com/michelle-sharon